Bless You!

*Restoring the
Biblically Hebraic
Blessing*

Restoration Foundation

Restoration Foundation is an international, transdenominational, multicultural teaching and publishing resource to the Christian community. This ministry features a network of scholars, church leaders, and laypersons who share the vision for restoring the Hebrew foundations of the Christian faith, promoting the unity of the Spirit among believers, and returning the church to a biblical relationship of loving support for the international Jewish community and the nation of Israel.

We publish *Restore!* magazine, a high-quality journal that features theological balance and scholarly research. *Restore!* helps Christians recover their Hebraic heritage while strengthening their faith in Jesus. We also publish and distribute *Golden Key Books*, a publishing effort that focuses exclusively on producing and marketing books and other materials that teach the various aspects of Christianity's Jewish roots.

We maintain an inspirational and informative Internet web site: *www.restorationfoundation.org*. Through this medium, we make much of our material available free of charge to people around the world. Entire issues of *Restore!* and volumes of *Golden Key Books* can be studied here.

Our team of *Golden Key Partners* around the world help us translate these various parts of our expansive vision into the programs that touch the lives of thousands. We invite you to join us as full partners in this teaching and publishing ministry. Together we are making a difference in the world by restoring Christians to their biblically Hebraic heritage, by eradicating Judaeophobia and anti-Semitism, by supporting Israel and the international Jewish community, and by encouraging unity among those who share this vision.

For information about Restoration Foundation, *Restore!* magazine, *Golden Key Books*, and *Golden Key Partnerships*, contact us at the address below.

Restoration Foundation
P. O. Box 421218
Atlanta, Georgia 30342, U.S.A.

www.restorationfoundation.org

Bless You!

Restoring the Biblically Hebraic Blessing

John D. Garr, Ph.D.

GOLDEN KEY BOOKS
Restoration Foundation
P. O. Box 421218
Atlanta, Georgia 30342, U.S.A.

*To my faithful friend and
colleague
Dr. Karl D. Coke
and his wife Karen
for blessing Pat and me
with their loving support
both in adversity
and in triumph.*

TABLE OF CONTENTS

Introduction

"Bless you!" is an oft-repeated phrase in today's world. When someone sneezes in public, others use this exclamation to wish him well. When Christians in various communions greet one another, they often repeat the phrase as a gesture of good will and good wishes. Very few, however, actually think that a blessing is conveyed, for such language and actions are merely social convention and expressions of concern and support.

In the ancient world, however, people routinely blessed one another. They shared mutual blessings over homes, children, land, labors, travels, and resources of every sort. Blessings were almost commonplace; however, they were certainly not meaningless. The ancients actually believed that something occurred when they blessed.

Much has been said about divine blessings (or the lack thereof) upon humanity. Universalists insist that all humanity–perhaps even all creation–is or will be eternally blessed by God. Some argue that blessings apply to certain people groups while other segments of the population live under eternal curses. Much of the Christian church asserts that God's blessing is essentially reserved for Christian believers. Whole segments of Christianity have been founded upon the idea that God is obligated to bless those who call upon him in faith. Some even suggest that God is at the beck and call of man with virtual on-demand blessings instantly available to those who understand and recite certain formulae.

What, then, is the biblical truth about the concept of blessing, and how should it be manifest among those who believe in God in today's world? Since divine blessing is such a vital concept, essential to mental, physical, and spiritual health, it is important that we "get it right." We must return to the source so that we can drink from the fountain of the water of life. Downstream sources are inevitably polluted and perhaps even poisoned. This is but another example of the truth that understanding the Hebrew foundations of Christian faith is a golden key that unlocks the treasures of Holy Scripture. Tapping into the Jewish roots of our faith is always an enriching, invigorating experience.

In order to have a clear and comprehensive understanding of divine blessing, then, we must return to the matrix from which the concept of blessing emerged. We must recover the Hebraic foundations of the blessing itself, of the one who blesses, and of the one who is blessed.

We can never have an accurate understanding of our Christian faith until we first know the Scriptures, history, and culture of the Jewish people in which Christianity is rooted. Unless we return to the Hebrew foundations of Christian concepts and applications, we will always be vulnerable to misconception, superstition, and exploitation.

It is for this reason that we have undertaken this volume in which we will discuss the biblical and historical background of the concept of blessing, the dynamics of the blessing process, applications of blessing, times for blessing, and reciprocity in blessing. We will also study the biblical emphasis on family blessings and their impact upon individuals and society. We will carefully examine the Jewish roots of the blessing experience so that we can more clearly understand both the concept and its applications. I am convinced that you will be amazed when you come to know the biblical background of the blessing and how it can impact your life and that of your family and community in powerful and enduring ways.

I would like to express my appreciation for the blessing of shared insight that has come to me from friends and colleagues in ministry and in academia. Foremost among these is my faithful friend, Dr. Karl D. Coke, president of Redirection Ministries, who has both blessed me personally and has shared invaluable insights into the dynamics of blessing. Others include Dr. Lynn Reddick, president of Open Church Ministries, who has made the study of blessing a passion that has enriched the lives of many around the world. I am also grateful to Dwight A. Pryor, president of the Center for Judaic-Christian Studies, and Dr. Marvin R. Wilson, Professor of Biblical Studies at Gordon College, for their incisive and inspiring teaching on aspects of this subject. I also give thanks to God for the superb help of Dr. Charles Bryant-Abraham and his wonderful wife Lu Ellen for their invaluable contributions of insight and wisdom and for their critique of the manuscript. I am likewise deeply indebted to Judy Grehan for her careful examination of the manuscript and for her thoughtful suggestions for its improvement both in content and style.

One thing we know for certain is that in a world filled with curses there is a profound need for blessing. There is a deep-seated hunger in the heart of all humanity for words of benediction to be spoken into lives pained by brokenness and loneliness. Evidence of this is that some 1,236 books on blessing are currently listed in Amazon.com. Many of these promote pagan ritual blessings from polytheism, pantheism, and other monist religions that only lead people further from the divine truth about blessing. I believe this volume will make a significant contribution to understanding the biblically Hebraic blessing that will bring true enrichment to lives of believers around the world.

I pray that as you read this book, you will be transported into a new dimension of blessing and being blessed. I trust also that this volume will generate in you a hunger for greater understanding of the heritage of our Christian faith that is deeply rooted in soil of biblical and Second Temple Judaism, the faith in which Jesus and the apostles lived their lives and expressed their devotion to God.

Understanding your faith in its original Hebraic context can be one of the greatest blessings in your life since the time that you came to faith in the living God and in his eternal provision for redemption, his Son, our Lord, Jesus Christ.

"The blessing of the Lord be upon you: we bless you in the name of the Lord."

In Messiah,
John D. Garr, Ph.D.

Chapter 1

Covenant
and Blessing

God's overwhelming determination to bless his people is captured in a profoundly succinct declaration from the pen of Paul in the introduction to his Ephesian letter. In language and formula typical to his fellow Jews of all ages, the rabbi from Tarsus, who had become the apostle to the Gentiles, exclaimed, "Blessed be the God and Father of our Lord Jesus Christ, who has blessed us with every spiritual blessing in the heavenly places in Christ."[1]

Two distinct Jewish traditions of the time were manifest in this statement. First, the apostle employed the ancient formula of *berakhot* (blessings), beginning his declaration by first blessing God. Jewish blessings to this day begin with the same exclamation that predates the Christian era: "*Barukh attah Adonai, Elohenu, Melekh haOlam.*" ("Blessed are you, O Lord our God, King of the universe.").[2] Paul no doubt understood that no blessing, prayer, or petition should be offered without first ascribing a blessing of praise to God himself, the giver of every good gift and blessing.

The second device that Paul used from his rabbinic heritage was the repetition of words, which in the Hebrew language is the means of adding emphasis. Comparatives and superlatives are created in this manner by repeating words and phrases. Paul's use of the same word three times in this statement underscores the utter blessedness of God's family. The God who blesses with every blessing is himself blessed through praise.

We know that God is a God of blessing today because it has always been a part of his nature to bless. Blessing did not begin with the Christian era as some have mistakenly supposed. God has always been the source of blessing. The biblical record is replete with the outpouring of divine blessings upon those who approached the Almighty in faith and obedience. God has always been the source of blessing.

Since Greek was the *lingua franca* of the Gentile peoples to whom Paul was writing, he used the Greek word εὐλογία (*eulogia*) for blessing. This word literally means "good word," and is the source of the English word *eulogy*. It was employed in the Septuagint version of the Hebrew Scriptures to translate the Hebrew verbal בְּרָכָה (*berakah*), the stem of which initiates every Jewish blessing. The use of this formula and style clearly underscores Paul's complete continuity with the Hebraic foundations of Christian faith. It also firmly anchors the Christian expectation of divine benediction on the blessings that God has unceasingly bestowed upon the Jewish people from the time that he confirmed his covenant with their father Abraham.

THE ABRAHAMIC BLESSING

The author of the Book of Hebrews succinctly described the foundational blessing upon which both Judaism and Christianity are anchored: "For when God made a promise to Abraham, because he could swear by no one greater, he swore by himself, saying, 'Surely blessing I will bless you, and multiplying I will multiply you.' "[3] The Hebrew idiom of repetition underscores God's resolute determination to bless and multiply Abraham.

The Abrahamic blessing also involves reciprocity and is all-inclusive. God declared, "I will bless you and make your name great: and you shall be a blessing."[4] Then the Eternal further promised that as a result of his blessing upon Abraham, "all the nations of the earth shall be blessed in him."[5]

Abraham, then, is the perfect paradigm of divine blessing. He was the first man with whom God made a personal covenant, electing him and his family to be the "Chosen People." Abraham was the first man whom God called his friend, the one to whom he revealed his secrets.[6] He was a man of pure faith and faithfulness. He was the object of a personal blessing that God would extend to all the families of the earth because his faith embraced the whole of humankind–past, present, and future. "God condescended to address a single man, choose him, and establish him as his blessing-point in the world. God's sacrificial intentions [were] to be fulfilled in the *hic et nunc* of this world."[7] The effective operation of the blessing for the patriarchs and their world is consequential to the divine intention to bless all of mankind.[8] The Abrahamic covenant was an everlasting covenant, the impact of which has only expanded to reach the entire world through its renewal and expansion through Jesus Christ.

A FOUNDATION FOR BLESSING

What were the reasons for this profound blessing that God bestowed upon Abraham, a blessing that would redound to all the nations of the earth? Why did this one man in history obtain God's favor to the degree that he became the "father of all [the faithful]"?[9] Why was the Creator of the universe not ashamed to be called this nomad's God?[10]

Abraham was a Babylonian by birth who was reared in Ur of the Chaldees. He had become a Syrian by nationality by the time he received his divine call. The nation of his birth epitomized the religion that vaunted itself against the knowledge of God. Indeed, the Babylonian civilization was largely foundational to the polytheism that characterized virtually all of the ancient world.

Jewish *aggadot* (traditions) suggest that young Abraham's father, Terah, was a stone carver who fashioned idol images worshiped in Babylon. At a very young age, Abraham received a divine revelation that there was only one God who was invisible and that all the gods of Babylon were not gods at all. One day when Abraham's father was away, the young lad took a hammer and smashed all the images except the largest. When his father returned, he was livid with his son for having destroyed so many months of hard work. "What have you done?" he demanded. "I didn't do it, Father, the big god did," Abraham explained. Angered all the more, Terah raged back at his son, "The big god is nothing but a piece of stone. It could not have destroyed all these other gods." Abraham replied, "You're right. These gods are nothing but stone. There is only one God who is invisible."[11]

It was through these events that Abraham, his wife Sarah, and his descendants received the understanding of ethical monotheism. This, no doubt, prompted them to leave Babylon and to journey to Haran in Syria where the family lived until Terah died. At that time, Abraham received this divine summons: "*Lekh lekhah*" ("Go for yourself"). Abraham was commanded by God to draw on the resources of his inner strength and go from among his kindred to the land where God would send him. Because of his absolute confidence in the God who had been revealed to him, Abraham immediately obeyed and crossed over the Euphrates River into what would become the Promised Land.

When Abraham heeded the divine call, he left his country and people to become an stranger in an unknown land. He was cut off from the blood and soil that bond family and society. He became a nomad. Both Abraham and Sarah were addressed as *gerim* (aliens), the term later applied to those who were not born Hebrews. He was as Gentile as it was possible to be.

FAITHFULNESS AND JUSTICE

By crossing the Euphrates, Abraham became the first Hebrew, and ultimately the first man to enter into a covenant with God to be his chosen. The word *Hebrew* is from the Hebrew word *eber*, which means "to cross over"; therefore, Abraham's crossing the Euphrates was the act of faith that transformed him from a Gentile into the first Hebrew.

It has been no coincidence that subsequent demonstrations of faith that have resulted in covenantal relationship have also involved crossing over or through the waters. Before Abraham's descendants became the nation of Israel at Sinai, they individually passed through the walled-up waters of the Reed Sea in a death, burial, and resurrection experience that Paul identified as a baptism.[12] John's baptism likewise involved leading the Israelites out into the Jordan, where they left the Promised Land behind, immersed themselves in the water, and turned again in true repentance (*teshuvah*) to the land of Israel.[13] When proselytes from the Gentiles were added to Israel, they immersed themselves in the waters of the *mikveh*.[14] When they broke the plane of the water in their own death, burial, and resurrection experience, they underwent a forensic change of status, actually becoming Jewish. Likewise, Christians partake of the same death, burial, and resurrection experience in baptism when they repent and are translated (carried across) from the kingdom of darkness into the kingdom of God's dear Son.[15] They, too, have crossed over and have become spiritual Hebrews, the children of Abraham.[16]

Abraham's immediate response to the divine imperative, "Go!", was the very essence of faith and faithfulness,[17] qualities that God accepted and credited to the man of faith for the righteousness that he did not inherently possess.[18] The status that Abraham achieved before God was based solely on his faith that was manifest in obedience to divine commands and his faithfulness to fulfill the just requirements of God's instructions.[19] Faith for Abraham was not static propositions and tenets; it remained a living, active, and dynamic faithfulness demonstrated in instantaneous response to further divine imperatives (e.g., Abraham set out early in the morning for the mountain of sacrifice when he was commanded to offer Isaac).

God's blessing on Abraham, therefore, was predicated entirely on his faith. His acceptance before God (salvation from pagan religion) was based solely in his confidence in one God, the faith upon which he acted.[20] God himself noted that Abraham had not only believed God but had also been obedient to his will. Decades later when God addressed Abraham's son, Isaac, he reiterated the solemn promise he had made in covenant with Abraham: "I will perform the oath which I swore unto Abraham your father. I will multiply your descendants as the stars of heaven, and will give your descendants all these lands; and by your descendants all the nations of the earth shall be blessed; because Abraham obeyed my voice, and kept my charge, my commandments, my statutes, and my laws."[21] It is remarkable that God commended Abraham for having kept all of his commandments, statutes, and laws over 400 years before those instructions were codified at Mt. Sinai as Israel's national constitution.

A second factor in Abraham's confidence and faithfulness that attracted God's attention and was also a basis for his call and the subsequent covenant of blessing was Abraham's faithfulness to transmit his faith and understanding to the generations after him. God observed this quality in Abraham: "I know that [Abraham] will command his children, and his household after him, and they shall keep the way of the Lord, to do justice and judgment; that the Lord may bring upon Abraham that which he hath spoken of him."[22] Not only was God pleased with Abraham's faith and its demonstration through positive actions of faithfulness, he was also pleased with Abraham's commitment to ensure that his faith was projected into future generations by teaching his family to observe God's ways by doing justice.

CHESED AND DEFERENCE

God's blessing on Abraham was also influenced by Abraham's Godlike quality of mercy and deference. The *chesed* of God, that virtually untranslatable quality of tender mercy and loving kindness, was continually manifest in Abraham's life and was an outworking of his faith and total dependence upon God. When Lot's herdsmen contended with Abraham's servants over pasturage rights, Abraham deferred to Lot, inviting him to select the part of the Promised Land that he wanted. Abraham knew that God had given him the entire land; therefore, he had no innate need to defend his property rights. He readily shared what appeared to be the best part of that land with his nephew.

Abraham manifest his spirit of deference again at the very moment when God was confirming his election and establishing the promise of Isaac's miraculous birth. Just as God was speaking the words Abraham most wanted to hear, the patriarch interrupted to exclaim, "Oh that Ishmael might live before you."[23] This petition was a profound incongruity! What was Abraham thinking? When he could have been totally focused on the fulfillment of his and his dear wife Sarah's lifelong dream, Abraham manifest divine *chesed* and deferred, sharing his concern for Ishmael, Hagar's son.

By then he had realized that Sarah's surrogate motherhood solution for the fulfillment of God's seemingly impossible promise of an Abrahamic heir had been a mistake. It was an error that God was about to remedy; however, the *chesed* in Abraham's heart cried out that Ishmael might be preserved, not just to life but to life before God or in God's presence. God's response was that the Abrahamic blessing was so powerful that it had reached the bondson as well.

Then, there was that occasion when God appeared to Abraham to inform his friend that he was about to rain down destruction on Sodom and Gomorrah. With the news of this impending disaster, Abraham could well have rejoiced that such an abominable people would soon be obliterated from the face of the earth. Like the disciples of Jesus, he could have insisted that God "rain down fire from heaven."[24] Instead, Abraham had the *chutzpah* to negotiate with God, offering various scenarios in which God could spare the evil cities. Abraham's deference interceded for the very epitome of evil in his time. Through this entire incident, Abraham engaged in prophetic intercession because he had been designated by God as the blessing-bearer to all humanity.[25] When not even a quorum of righteous ones (ten, the number of the *minyan*) could be found, Abraham relented, and God destroyed those evil cities.[26]

THE PERFECT STATE FOR BLESSING

It could well be said that Abraham fully realized the formula that the prophet Micah two millennia later would set forth for the process of walking humbly with God: doing justice and loving mercy.[27] He did justice through faith, and he imparted these qualities transgenerationally. At the same time, he also loved and manifested *chesed* and deference. In this way, Abraham fulfilled God's instruction to him that he walk in perfection before God.[28] Abraham was no superhuman figure. He had his faults and failures. He did, however, walk before God in תָּמִים (*tamim*), the perfection that is more clearly defined as "uprightness, wholeness, without blemish, and having integrity."

While from the perspective of historical Christian perfectionism, the ideal state for the believer has been viewed as having reached a certain plateau of conduct that is considered "above sin" or sinless, the biblically Hebraic idea of perfection (*tamim*) is that of having a spirit of constant improvement, of moving nearer to God in *imitatio Dei*, con-

forming oneself to the will of God and the mind of Christ.
Having the *spirit* of perfection protects one from being inflated with the pride of self-righteousness that the *status* of
perfection often produces. It helps one understand that only
God is perfect and that everyone else is becoming. The *spirit*
of perfection impels one forward to greater faith in God's
provision of *chesed* for right motive and right conduct.

It was on the basis of faithfulness and deference that Jesus
insisted that his countrymen should do the works of Abraham
if they were to claim the patriarch as their father.[29] It was also
on this foundation for blessing that the Master urged his disciples to "be perfect, just as your Father in heaven is perfect,"[30]
an injunction that he made in the context of his commandment to manifest pure *chesed* by loving their enemies and giving to the poor. Integrity and uprightness according to the
divine model enable believers to love and serve enemies, pat-
terning their *chesed* after God himself who so loved the human race that he gave his Son's life to redeem and bless those
who were alienated from him. It also impels them to manifest
acts of loving kindness to the needy of society.

These qualities provide a perfect foundation for God's
blessing. And, God will always bless those who are upright
with true integrity. He will also bless those who insist on
the justice of God in their own lives, in the lives of others,
and in society in general. He will fully bless those who
manifest loving kindness in deference to others and who
transfer the blessing that he has given them into a blessing for their fellow man.

BLESSING WHAT GOD HAS BLESSED

Because Abraham was blessed by God, he could be
and was blessed by men. Melchizedek, the righteous royal
priest of Salem, blessed Abraham when he offered the tithe
of his increase to God after he had defeated Lot's kidnap-
pers. Melchizedek said, "Blessed be Abram of the most high
God . . . and blessed be the most high God. . ."[31] Some

Jewish sages have questioned why Melchizedek blessed Abraham before he blessed God. The truth is that as God's priest he merely affirmed what he knew God had already done. He blessed the one whom God had blessed.

God's blessing in one's life will result in the addition of men's blessings. Melchizedek spoke good things into the life of the man whom God had blessed. Balaam realized that he could only bless what God had blessed,[32] even though he had been hired to curse Israel. Solomon declared that "a man's gift (from God) makes room for him and brings him before great men."[33]

A BLESSING TO BLESS

Abraham was not blessed by God solely for his own personal benefit. Of the patriarch, God said, "I will bless you . . . and multiply your children,"[34] and "in you all the families of the earth shall be blessed,"[35] and "in your seed all the nations of the earth shall be blessed."[36] First, the blessing was given to Abraham, then to his physical descendants, and finally to all the nations of the world. God's immediate intention was to bless the one individual whom he had found with the faith to believe and, without hesitation, to act upon His Word. His long-term intentions, however, were to bless all the progeny of the Edenic family that he had blessed in the beginning.

Since God is the Eternal, the one who dwells in the forever present, the final denouement of the ages is and has always been of immediate concern to him. For the Eternal, the past, present, and future coexist. The final end has already occurred. Since God is eternal, he is already there as well as here in man's now. This is why it is said that God declares "the end from the beginning."[37] He can do this because he *is* the *Aleph* and the *Tav*, the *Alpha* and the *Omega*, the beginning and the end.[38] God's ultimate concern is the same as it was in the beginning. He blessed humanity then, he continues to bless humanity, and his final act for humanity will be one of blessing.

God's choice of Abraham because of his faithfulness was to become a dynamic model to the nations of the benefits that result from following God's instructions. God would use the one whom he had blessed to become a channel of blessing for all men. Through Abraham, the chosen people would come forth who would be God's witnesses in the world,[39] a manifestation of his light to the nations.[40] Ultimately, through Abraham's progeny, the one would be born who would personify the light[41] by being the fullness of divinity incarnate.[42] He would draw humanity to himself and restore them to God by imputing to them his own personal righteousness for their faith. Then in the final judgment, he would bless the nations of the redeemed by saying to them, "Come, you blessed of my Father, inherit the kingdom prepared for you from the foundation of the world."[43]

The blessedness of the Abrahamic family was not, therefore, for their personal aggrandizement. It was not a divine scheme to develop a super race of demigods. It was not to enlist a super power that would dominate the world and thereby enslave the masses in robotic obeisance both to themselves and to their God. The blessedness of the first Hebrew and all subsequent Hebrews was for serving the world with enlightenment and blessing.

BLESSING AND CURSE

What God has blessed will forever remain blessed. All efforts at removing the blessing or at cursing the ones whom God has blessed ultimately result in disaster.[44] God made this promise to Abraham: "I will bless those that bless you, and I will curse him that curses you."[45] Since a curse or malediction is the opposite of a blessing or benediction, God does not allow anyone to work in opposition to his purposes without inviting his judgment. When God blesses, it is a divine act that neither evil forces nor any man can reverse. When anyone attempts to subvert God's blessing by bringing forth imprecations against those whom God has blessed, their curses are deflected by the aura of grace that surrounds God's elect. Along with God's curse, they are returned to their source with devastating results.

First, God said, "I will curse him that curses you." It is interesting that the singular is used in relationship to the *one* who curses while the plural is used for those who bless. Perhaps God intended to point out that the source of all curses is *haSatan*, the accuser of the brethren,[46] who has been cursed by the Almighty since the angelic rebellion. That curse was reinforced following Satan's deception that effected the subversion of Adam and Eve.[47] The enemy of men's souls ever formulates curses against those who are the objects of God's love and blessing; however, God's curse will ultimately destroy him.

Second, God curses nations and people who curse his chosen and blessed people. To confirm this fact, one needs only to observe in the anals history those nations that have dared to touch the pupil (apple) of God's eye, the children of Abraham.[48] Every power that has exalted itself against the Hebrews and their descendants, the Jews, has met with crushing defeat. Even those nations that had enjoyed God's blessing felt the sting of God's curse when they turned their backs upon the chosen people. A litany of examples could be cited of once-proud kingdoms of extensive political and military might that were reduced to ruin because they dared to harm God's blessed ones, a clear lesson for modern relationships with the Jewish people.

Third, God curses individuals who direct their malevolence against those whom he has blessed. The record of Holy Scripture is replete with references of those who met ruin because they stretched forth their hands to touch God's anointed ones.[49] This is why it is so important that believers today exercise great care in how and whom they judge and target for imprecations. Excoriation and anathema should be rarely used, if at all. One can never be sure whether or not he is cursing one whom God has blessed. How can curses and blessings come from the same mouth?[50] The tongue, the body's most untamed member, must be restrained.[51] This is why there is far more scriptural admonition about judging and speaking evil of one another than about precise standards for personal conduct.[52]

MATERIAL BLESSING BENEFITS

As seen in the Abrahamic covenant, divine blessing was more than an expression of approval: it carried with it material benefits.[53] As Abraham proceeded into the land to which God had directed him, he was given progressively increasing divine promises about that land. First God said, "I will give you this land."[54] Then he declared that all that Abraham's eyes could see would be his.[55] Subsequently he promised that through his family Abraham would inherit the land from the river of Egypt to the Euphrates.[56] Finally the Apostolic Scriptures confirm that, through the one who would be the fullest manifestation of both the Son of Abraham[57] and the Son of God,[58] the patriarch would inherit the world."[59] Abraham's faith so pleased God that both the blessing and the promise were ever expanded and more clearly defined.

The transgenerational nature of God's promises is apparent in the fulfillment of God's blessing of Abraham. The patriarch himself never inherited the land and actually owned only a small plot for a family cemetery. The inheritance he was promised was given to his descendants four centuries later. Even then, the chosen people, the children of Abraham, did not inherit the fullness of the promise. Ultimately, the divine real estate contract will not come to fruition until the Son of promise, the Lord Jesus, returns to inherit the entire earth as God's dominion.[60]

The blessing, then, was more than an ethereal, heavenly promise: it was an entitlement to real property, to tangible assets in a real world. In reality, Abraham needed only a burial plot because he knew a resurrection was coming! The city for which he spent a lifetime searching[61] is the same one that John saw coming to earth in the Messianic Kingdom.[62] At that time God's original real estate transaction with Abraham will be fulfilled when both the patriarch and all his children, both natural and spiritual, will sit down with the Son of Abraham, the Son of God, in the everlasting kingdom.[63]

The material aspects of the Abrahamic covenant and blessing demonstrate the fact that God's blessing is not just a spiritual exercise. God's blessing provides material benefits as well. This fact underscores the Hebraic truth that not only does heaven belong to God but also, "the earth is the Lord's, and the fulness thereof."[64] Man's existence is a holistic experience that involves every aspect of life, including both the spiritual and the material. From the sublime to the mundane, everything is spiritual, and everything is theological.[65] This is a profound Hebraic truth that diametrically confronts the Hellenistic dualism that posits the spiritual in opposition to the material and promotes the ideal state as escape from the evil material world and absorption into the spiritual heavenly realm. In the biblically Hebraic perspective, the earth is good because it was created good[66] and it will be the habitation of the righteous forever,[67] even when there is a new earth wherein dwells righteousness.[68]

Because of the infiltration of Hellenism's Gnostic and Platonic philosophies into the church through many of its Greek and Latin fathers, many Christians of history have desperately sought detachment from the earthy and the material. As a result, they have viewed the Jewish people as carnal and materialistic. In reality, the Jews were right! They merely maintained spiritual *and* material expectation of blessing from the Abrahamic covenant. For them, the earth was good, and all the good in it was to be enjoyed within the parameters of God's instructions.

Throughout the four millennia of their participation in

that archetypal covenant, the Hebrews have concerned them-selves with the earthly inheritance and its accompanying re-sponsibilities. They have seen themselves as "keepers of the garden,"[69] working in partnership with God in *tikkun olam*, the restoration of the world.

A UNILATERAL COVENANT

God's covenant with Abraham was not bilateral. It was not predicated upon Abraham's performance. It was secured solely in God's immutable oath. God did not say, "If you will do . . . I will . . ." He simply declared, "I will establish my covenant between me and you and your descen-dants after you."[70]

Though Abraham believed God and had his belief credited to him for the righteousness (rightness, ethical con-duct) that he did not innately possess; though Abraham was faithful to fulfill all of God's ethical requirements; and though Abraham was filled with the divine *chesed*, of mercy, of compassion, and of deference; in the final analysis, the Abrahamic covenant was unilateral and was based solely in God's commitment to Abraham and his descendants. It was confirmed by God's inviolable oath[71] and established on his immutable promise.[72]

Men can never hope to earn God's favor. It is freely bestowed out of divine love. The blessing is based in God's initiative and in the unconditional grace of his promise.[73] Though man returns God's blessing to the Creator as thanksgiving, the blessing is unilateral. God simply is, he says, and he does!

[1] Ephesians 1:3.
[2] Because the adjective *barukh* is the same verbal form as *hannun* ("gracious" or "overflowing with grace") and *rahum* ("merciful" or "over-flowing with mercy"), *barukh attah* could more accurately be rendered, "overflowing with blessing are you."
[3] Hebrews 6:13-14.
[4] Genesis 12:2.
[5] Genesis 18:18.

[6] 2 Chronicles 20:7, Isaiah 41:8, and James 2:23 speak of Abraham as God's friend. John 15:15 states that Jesus called his disciples "friends" because he revealed his secrets to them.

[7] J.T.E. Renner, " 'Believing' in the Beginning of Blessing-History," *Lutheran Theological Journal* 20 (1986), p. 49.

[8] William Yarchin, "Imperative and Promise in Genesis 12:1-3," *Studia Biblical et Theologica* 10 (1980), pp. 164-178.

[9] Romans 4:11, 16.

[10] Matthew 22:32.

[11] This is a paraphrase of the story.

[12] 1 Corinthians 10:2.

[13] Mark 1:4-5.

[14] The *mikveh* was a pool of living water (from rainfall, a spring, or a stream) that was used for ceremonial ablutions.

[15] Colossians 1:13.

[16] Romans 4:16; Galatians 3:29.

[17] *Emunah*, the Hebrew word translated "faith," is more accurately rendered "faithfulness."

[18] Genesis 15:6; Romans 4:3.

[19] James 2:23-24.

[20] The Abrahamic salvific experience of deliverance from paganism is replicated in all believers, who are delivered from the power of sin and are brought into God's kingdom solely on the basis of their faith–their confidence in God's loving kindness. Believers are saved today in exactly the same manner as Abraham was: God accepts their faith and credits it for righteousness, the imputed personal righteousness of Jesus Christ.

[21] Genesis 26:3-5, RSV.

[22] Genesis 18:19, KJV.

[23] Genesis 17:18, NASB.

[25] H. W. Wolf, quoted in Renner, " 'Believing' in the Beginnings of Blessing-History," p. 53.

[26] Genesis 18:32, 19:24-25.

[27] Micah 6:8.

[28] Genesis 17:1.

[29] John 8:39.

[30] Matthew 5:48, NASB.

[31] Genesis 14:19, KJV.

[32] Numbers 23:20.

[33] Proverbs 18:16.

[34] Genesis 22:17.

[35] Genesis 12:3.

[36] Genesis 22:18.

[37] Isaiah 46:10.

[38] Revelation 21:6; 22:13.

[39] Isaiah 43:10.

[40] Isaiah 42:6; 49:6.

[41] John 1:4.

[42] Colossians 2:9.

[43] Matthew 25:34.

[44] The prime example of the disastrous results of cursing what God has blessed is found in Balaam who ultimately lost his life as a result of attempting to curse Israel. In reality Balaam's donkey was wiser than the prophet.

[45] Genesis 12:3.

[46] Revelation 12:10.

[47] Genesis 3:14.

[48] Zechariah 2:8.

[49] Psalm 105:15.

[50] James 3:10.

[51] James 3:5-8.

[52] Romans 14:3, 4; James 4:11.

[53] Pamela J. Scalise, "The Significance of Curses and Blessings," *Biblical Illustrator* 13 (Fall 1986), pp. 57-59.

[54] Genesis 12:7.

[55] Genesis 13:14, 15.

[56] Genesis 15:18.

[57] Matthew 1:1.

[58] John 1:18.

[59] Romans 4:13.

[60] Luke 22:29; Psalm 2:7-9; Zechariah 14:9.

[61] Hebrews 11:10.

[62] Revelation 21:2.

[63] Matthew 8:11.

[64] Psalm 24:1, KJV.

[65] Marvin R. Wilson, *Our Father Abraham: Jewish Roots of the Christian Faith* (Grand Rapids: Wm. B. Eerdmans, 1989), p.176.

[66] Genesis 1:10.

[67] Psalm 37:9-11; 115:16.

[68] 2 Peter 3:13; Revelation 21:1.

[69] Genesis 2:15.

[70] Genesis 17:7.

[71] Hebrews 6:13.

[72] Hebrews 6:17.

[73] Frederick W. Bush, "Images of Israel: The People of God in the Torah," *Studies in Old Testament Theology*, p. 108.

Chapter 2

Original Blessing

Despite God's eternal commitment to bless mankind, Christianity has focused its theology for centuries on the theme of the fall and redemption. For all practical purposes, its anthropology begins with the Edenic sin of Adam, the defining moment in the history of the human race. Indeed, the Holy Scriptures make it clear that all men are slaves to sin.[1] King David lamented the sinful condition that had produced his unspeakable iniquity: "I was born with iniquity; with sin my mother conceived me."[2] The Apostle Paul shared the pain of sin's addiction: "The good that I would I do not: but the evil which I would not, that I do."[3] The record is clear, "There is none righteous, no not one."[4]

The purpose of the incarnation of Jesus, therefore, was to deliver mankind from the hopeless abyss of enslavement to sin.[5] If it were not for sin, there would be no need for a Savior. This, therefore, is the great mystery of why God was manifest in the flesh[6] in the incarnation of Jesus, so that he might be tempted with all sins common to man and overcome them,[7] subsequently to be sacrificed to atone for humanity's sins and to be resurrected in triumph over sin and death.[8] Now, as a result of the Messiah's finished work of redemption, all who come to faith in Jesus are delivered from the power of sin and become ambassadors for Christ, saying to the world, "Be reconciled to God."[9]

Humanity's liberation from sin, however, is nought but the consummation of God's unending commitment to mankind for covenant and blessing. From the very foundation of the world, his eternal plan provided for redemption through the sacrificed Lamb of God who takes away the sin of the world.[10] Redemptive history is, therefore, a history of blessing.[11] Adam's fall was foreseen, and provision was made before the fall to recover, secure, and fulfill the covenant and blessing. The life, death, and resurrection of Jesus merely provided the means by which the covenant and blessing could be fully restored to mankind. God, therefore, has never been fixated on man's sin: he has always been committed to man's blessing.

ORIGINAL SIN

For centuries, the corporate and individual psyches of Christians have been focused on the first sin of mankind. This should come as no surprise, for even the apostles of Jesus at times seemed to be preoccupied with sin. When a man afflicted with congenital blindness sought healing from the hand of Jesus, the disciples were more concerned with whether the man's condition had been precipitated by his sin or his parents' sin. The church's fixation contrasted with the mind of Christ could not be more clearly demonstrated. Replying to his followers' sin interrogative, Jesus declared, "Neither . . . but that the works of God should be made revealed in him."[12] The blindness was simply an opportunity for God's grace to be manifest in blessing. Sin had nothing to do with it.

Perhaps it is a very human trait to be focused on sin rather than on blessing. It is a simple fact of media theory that "bad news sells." People are much more drawn to danger, to the sinister, to disaster, to evil personified than they are to good news about good deeds. Could it be that this condition is a testament to the fallen state of man? Mankind in general is given to criticism even of good, to paroxysms of anger, to expectations of gloom and doom. The good and blessedness in the lives of others are generally overlooked in the preoccupation with muckraking for the bad. The shining gold is always unperceived in the unending quest to dig up the dirt.

It was Augustine, the Latin theologian from northern Africa, who posited the idea of "Original Sin." There were precursors to this concept in the teachings of various ante-Nicene fathers of the church. Augustine himself cited eleven of these fathers as supporting his thesis.[13] Most prominent among them were Tertullian and Origen. Influenced by the materialistic monism of the Montanist cult, Tertullian, the Latin polemicist, taught that sin is a physical taint that is propagated generationally through procreation. Origen, the Greek allegorist, believed in the preexistence of the souls of men before the creation of the present world as spirits without material bodies, an idea consistent with his preconversion status as a neo-Platonist philosopher. He was further convinced that the material world was created so that these spirits could be disciplined and purified in order that ultimate reconciliation could be accomplished, with all men and even the devil eventually restored to God.[14] Origen also supposed that a hereditary sin originated in Adam and was transmitted through the pollution and sinfulness of sexual union. This idea had been suggested as early as the first century in the fourth Book of Esdras, which asserts that Adam transmitted to all his posterity the malignity of the bad seed of sin.[15]

It was Augustine, however, who set forth the theology of Original Sin, defending his views in 418 A.D. in "*De Gratia Christi et de peccato originali*" ("Of the Grace of Christ and of original sin"). Augustine advanced the premise that by virtue of organic unity, the entire human race existed in Adam and shared in his will to rebel against God so that the very nature of mankind was corrupted by Adam's sin.

Systematic theologian Louis Berkhof sums up this concept: "Every man is guilty in Adam, and is consequently born with a depraved and corrupt nature."[16]

Augustine's theology was also influenced by a neo-Platonist world view that conceived of matter as essentially evil. Earlier in his career, he had been involved in Manichaeism, a cult whose Gnostic dualism prompted them to view all matter as evil and led them to claim that Christ was never incarnate in flesh, that he did not die, nor did he resurrect from the dead. Their extreme monophysitism sought to destroy the only precondition for the scriptural doctrine of salvation, the humanity of Jesus, the Jew.[17]

Augustine further argued, as had Origen before him, that Adam's sin was transmitted to all his descendants from generation to generation by the lust of sexual conjugation so that all human beings were considered sinners from the moment of conception. For Augustine, it was sexual concupiscence that was the root of the primal rebellion, original sin. Though he generally argued that all sin is voluntary ("*omne peccatum ex voluntate*"), he did make one exception for *natura vitiata* (a sin which belongs to nature and not to the sphere of the human will). The only involuntary sin was sexual desire, the lust of procreation. Everything related to human sexuality was for this church father inherently sinful, from the first glimmer of desire until final orgasm. Even matrimonial conjugation, though permitted by Paul, was inherently sinful. The original sin that was transmitted from Adam to mankind through sexual generation made all humans inherently sinners from the moment of conception. Taken to its logical end, this argument even asserted that all unbaptized infants are damned.[18]

Whatever the case may be, the imprint of Augustinian thought on Christian theology has been indelible. Though Eastern Orthodoxy did not recognize the doctrine of original sin (probably because Augustine's writings were not translated from Latin into Greek until many centuries after his death), virtually all of the Western church accepted Augustine's teaching. Many variations on his idea of original sin have been presented over the centuries, and the great controversies that arose in Augustine's day over the related doctrines of divine sovereignty, predestination, and man's free will have continued until the present time.

PREDESTINATION VS. FREE WILL

From the time of Augustine, much of the church has believed that the sovereignty of God required the absolute predestination of man. This Augustinian theology undergirded much of the Reformation, particularly Calvinism, founded by John Calvin on the Swiss reformation led by Hulderich Zwingli. Calvinism championed this teaching, even taking it to its logical extreme in Supralapsarian Calvinism, which posited that before all creation, God predetermined for all time those individuals who would be saved and those who would be damned.

In the Synod of Dordt in 1618, the Calvinist position was set forth in five points, which have been outlined in order, using the word *tulip* as an acronym. These points were (1) total hereditary depravity, (2) unconditional election, (3) limited atonement, (4) irresistible grace, and (5) perseverance of the saints.

Foundational to the Calvinist theology of absolute predestination is the concept of total hereditary depravity. When this concept is carried to extreme, it asserts that because of man's depraved nature, he must forever commit sin, a seeming contradiction to Paul's assertion that believers should not continue in sin so that God's grace may abound.[19]

The questions of divine sovereignty and free will have been a subject of great debate among Christian theologians. If God predestined the elect and the damned, why was there a need for the proclamation of the gospel so that "whosoever will may come."[20] Pockets of resistance to the extremes of predestination teaching, therefore, have always existed. Controversies have abounded in history over these issues, with Augustine embattled with his chief protagonist, the early Celtic Christian theologian Pelagius, who followed in the teaching of Theodore of Mopsuestia in denying that the sin of Adam was the origin of death in humanity.

The issue of the juxtaposition of divine sovereignty with human free will has also perplexed Christian theologians for centuries. This battle raged after the Reformation as Lutherans and Calvinists debated Arminians, the followers of Jacobus Arminius who championed the doctrine of man's free will, insisting on the exercise of man's free will to choose whether he would serve God or not. Arminius declared that God determined to save believers by grace adapted to their free will, not by an omnipotent action that was not subject to their will.[21]

Some have argued that there is no such thing as original inherited sin so that at birth every human is given a *"tabula rasa"* (a blank slate) on which he may write either good or evil, all determined by his own free will. They believed, however, that in man's fallen state it is only God's grace that enables man to do the good and shun the evil.

Polarization over primeval events and their consequences for all subsequent humanity has often generated more heat than light. One extreme visualized mankind as totally depraved, irrevocably sinful, and forever damned except for divine intervention. The other posited an inherently good humanity that was victimized by temptation and sin and was, therefore, in need of redemption. Pitched battles have been waged for centuries, and human beings have been ostracized, excoriated, anathematized, and even murdered over these issues.

As is the case with most polarized issues, the truth is generally somewhere between the extremes. Ignoring the "proof texts" of opposing positions while championing one's own set of biblical citations does not facilitate a search for truth. It betrays instead a certain effete arrogance, an elitist attitude, a commitment to "being right" rather than seeking truth. The root of this problem has been the Christian preoccupation with "systematic theology," in which it is believed that everything in theology can be arranged in neat black-and-white categories. Everything that does not fit is either wrong or is simply ignored.

A HEBRAIC VIEW OF HUMAN NATURE

This is why the Hebraic understanding of theology in which the earliest Christian church was rooted is so important. It is striking that there has never been a "systematic theology" in the history of Judaism. The Jews have understood that there are many things about God and his relationship with mankind that cannot be understood with the rational mind. Some things must be held in dynamic tension so that on the one hand something is true while on the other, something else is also true. This is the case with the historical and theological fact of Adam's fall and its impact upon subsequent humanity, as well as with the issues of divine sovereignty in predestination and the free will of mankind.

The Jewish understanding of the subject posits that while in the womb all human beings possess a complete understanding of God's Word (Torah). At birth, however, each person becomes a "living soul" like Adam, loses the understanding of the Word, and receives a *yetzer hara*, an inclination toward evil. The *yetzer hara* is usually translated "evil imagination" and is characterized as evil, the enemy, and a stumbling-block.[22] The *yetzer hara* is the natural survival instinct that is wholly governed by self-interest. While it is the element in the human entity that produces evil, it, like everything else that God has created, has some good. Without it, one would not work, create a family, or otherwise develop.

From infancy, a child is wholly driven by self-interest which, if unchecked, ultimately produces evil (rebellion

against God). This truth is seen in the fact the "imagination
of man's heart is evil from his youth."[23] The sages, however,
have suggested that at puberty a child also receives a *yetzer
hatov*, an inclination for good.[24] The *yetzer hatov* represents
a return of commitment to the understanding of God's
Word (Torah) that was lost at birth. In effect, it represents
a reawakening to the Torah that was always written on the
heart.[25] For all subsequent human existence, a battle rages
between the two inclinations, perhaps the conflict which
Paul lamented in his own life that produced evil even when
he struggled to do good.[26] It may also be what Paul described as demolishing strongholds and "casting down imagi-
nations . . . bringing every thought into captivity to the
obedience of Christ."[27]

Though inevitably entangled in the web of sin because
of the inclination toward evil that accompanies his birth,
man is endowed with a drive toward good, a truth that is
underscored in the Hebrew Scriptures. Adam was made in
God's image.[28] This does not, however, suggest that man's
physical features were the same as God's, for God is incorporeal. God is Spirit. The anthropomorphisms and
theriomorphisms which mankind and even the Holy Scriptures attribute to God are simply metaphors by which they
can understand and relate to God. Man's creation in the
likeness of God is manifest in the fact that into man alone
the Creator imbued the "breath of life" (*neshamah*).[29]

The essence of what is "God breathed,"[30] the very words
of God,[31] was infused by God into Adam's nostrils and into
every subsequent human being. God's Word, his divine instruction (often called "the law"), has been written on the hearts
of all humans so that their consciences either condemn or excuse them.[32] The breath of the Almighty (*neshamah*) gives the
spirit (*nephesh*) of man understanding,[33] enlightening his life
with the lamp of the Divine Word.[34] It is the hearing of the
Word that generates faith in man's heart for salvation and
return to God.[35] Creating faith is entirely God's activity; he

alone speaks his word to man in this world.[36]

Subsequent biblical citations help us understand that though man is "shapen in iniquity,"[37] he is also "fashioned" by God's hands.[38] "It is [God] who has made us, and not we ourselves."[39] God formed man's spirit in him.[40] Of some, it was even said that they were called of God from the time they were in the womb.[41] Paul declares that man is the image and glory of God,[42] while James observes that men are made after the similitude of God.[43]

Has medical science demonstrated the fact that a spark of the divine rests in the heart of every man?[44] When an echocardiogram of the human heart is made, the tissues that separate the chambers of the heart are aligned in such a way as to manifest the Hebrew letter *shin* (ש). Throughout Judaism, this letter of the Hebrew alphabet is used as a symbol for God, for it is the first letter of the name *Shaddai* (the Almighty), one of the significant names applied to God in the Hebrew Scriptures. The letter *shin* appears on virtually every mezuzah, the box affixed to the doorposts of Jewish homes that contains a parchment inscribed with the Hebrew text of God's command that the Torah be written on the doorposts of all Israelite houses.[45] Is this merely a curious coincidence, or is it possible that God has left the imprint of his name on the very heart of every human being? Indeed, there is a spark of the divine in all

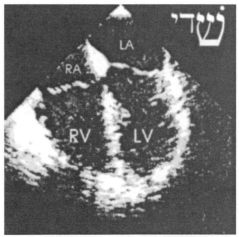

Graphic by Dr. William P. Cheshire

Echocardiogram of human heart clearly reveals the Hebrew letter ש (*shin*), the first letter of one the most ancient of God's names, *El Shaddai*.

people that ever draws them toward God and the good. If man bears a physical imprint of God in his heart, he certainly has an inclination toward good as well. Though the heart is deceitful and desperately wicked so that only God can know it,[46] the Eternal has maintained a spark in the heart of all men that can become a torch of enlightenment through the word of faith.[47]

Scriptural language speaks of the heart as though there are two hearts in man, the mind (the seat of the intellect) and the conscience (the seat of emotion and will). The problem for most people is that the mind dominates all they do, limiting what can be accomplished by the Spirit that indwells the heart. Such was the case with the disciples who were traveling from Jerusalem to Emmaus following the crucifixion of Jesus.[48] They were operating wholly within the rational realm and were exceedingly disappointed that their hopes had not been fulfilled. When Jesus joined them, he listened to their rationalizations and upbraided them as "slow of heart to believe all that the prophets have spoken." These disciples did not have a mental deficiency; they had a heart problem.

As Jesus proceeded to teach these disciples God's Word their "hearts burned" within them. Apparently, Jesus succeeded in connecting their minds with their hearts so that the Word of God could generate in them the faith to believe God's Word. After these disciples reported their experience to the apostles in Jerusalem, Jesus appeared to all and "opened their minds so they could understand the Scriptures."[49] He taught them from each portion of the Hebrew Scriptures (*TaNaKh*): the law (the *Torah*), the prophets (the *Nevi'im*), and the Psalms (the first book of the *Ketuvim*). The opening of their minds was a process of speaking the Scriptures to braid or plait together a threefold cord of mind, heart, and the Word of God to produce an unbreakable lifeline of faith.[50]

The human heart, then, has the potential to be impacted by the Word of God, the divine instructions that have been written to some degree in the conscience of every human. Of course, there is always the possibility that the conscience can become seared to the point that one becomes depraved and delusional and, therefore, unaffected by the divine call.[51] This, however, is the exception rather than the rule. While there is evil in every heart, there is also a spark of the divine that ever woos humanity toward relationship with God and obedience to his Word.

A BALANCED ANTHROPOLOGY

Judaism, then, does not exempt mankind from an inclination toward evil; however, neither does it posit that human beings are totally depraved and utterly incapable of good. The Hebraic understanding of the human condition begins from a more ancient event than the fall of man through the sin of rebellion. It works out its understanding from the point of God's "very good" (*tov me'od*) creation and the Eternal's covenant of blessing for this crowning creation, humankind.

This Hebraic perspective represents a balanced view between the extreme position of some who assert that each human being is born with a *tabula rasa* and is inherently good and pure and the other extreme that maintains that all humanity is inherently depraved, wholly incapable of good in themselves. It recognizes the consequences of the fall and the resultant inclination toward sin that is present in all humans while at the same time affirming the nature of man as reflecting the image of God and having an inclination toward good that results from the Torah engraved on his heart.

The theological debate over predestination and free will is also somewhat resolved when one adopts the Hebraic method of holding complex and polarized issues in dynamic tension. This allows for a middle-ground position that acknowledges God's absolutely sovereignty with the power to predetermine all things. On the other hand, it also recognizes that if man is to love God freely, he must do so out of free

will. In order to permit man the power to choose out of his
own free will, God limits his own sovereignty in much the
same way in which he limited his deity to the faculties of
humanity when he became man in the person of Jesus.
In this case, God predetermines his will for mankind
but permits individuals to exercise free will to choose
what course they will follow.

ORIGINAL BLESSING

Rather than being preoccupied with original sin, therefore, the Hebrews have focused on original blessing. God's
original intent for all of his creation was blessing. He is a God
who dispenses blessings, and he has demonstrated that he will
move all of heaven and earth to actualize his divine blessing.
God is not fixated on sin. He has an unrelenting preoccupation with blessing.

God first blessed the animal creation.[52] Then he blessed
Adam and Eve.[53] In the best tradition of the word *blessing*,
he spoke good words (Greek: *eulogia*) into their lives. It
might even be said that God's blessing to Adam and Eve
was the everlasting good news that the crowning creation
was to have dominion over all the earth,[54] for the gospel
that was conveyed to Abraham,[55] to Israel,[56] to the prophets,[57] to the apostles,[58] and to all believers[59] is that God's
kingdom (dominion) would come to earth and be given to
his chosen people.[60] The covenant of God has always
included a land contract of earthly dominion, leading
ultimately to the Messianic kingdom that will encom-
pass the entire earth.[61]

Even God's banishment of the progenitors of the
human race from the Garden of Eden was a blessing.
Here is God's reason for barring mankind from the
Garden: ". . . lest he put out his hand and take also of the
tree of life, and eat, and live forever. . ."[62] What seemed as
divine judgment was actually divine mercy. The *chesed* of God
was manifest when he protected Adam and Eve from eating

of the tree of life and becoming eternal sinners with no hope of redemption (like the fallen angels who are reserved in chains of darkness forever[63]). This is but a clear manifestation of the truth that God's justice and mercy are not in opposition to one another but are rather two views of God's one nature.

God is not schizophrenic, with one personality of judgment, wrath, and vindictiveness and another personality of love, grace, and mercy. God is love, and everything about his person and his actions is an outgrowth of his essence. The apostle John, because of his close relationship with Jesus,[64] likely had the clearest understanding of theology and Christology of anyone in his time. He summed up his understanding of God in this manner: "God is love."[65] Though God is often thought of in terms of judgment and is viewed as an austere judge just waiting to impose penalties, he is truly a lover, the lover of men's souls. God's love is so great as to be incomprehensible to man. God so loved that he gave himself in the person of his Son to save humanity. The salvation that came to man through Jesus Christ was not a product of God's judgment. It was a manifestation of his unfathomable love. "In this is love, not that we loved God, but that he loved us and sent his Son to be the propitiation for our sins."[66]

It is unfortunate that Christianity has often viewed God in terms of divine schizophrenia. From the time of Marcion, the first great Christian heretic in the early second century, the heavenly Father has been posited as stern, unyielding, and eager to judge, while the Son has been viewed as eternally epitomizing grace and mercy. The truth is that the Father "so loved the world that he gave his only begotten Son" not "to condemn the world, but that the world through him might be saved."[67]

There is no record of the abrogation of God's original Edenic blessing upon mankind. When man sinned, God cursed the serpent,[68] and he cursed the ground[69] because of Adam and Eve. Hardship and labor were to come upon man and woman because of their sin;[70] however, God did not curse Adam and Eve. The Creator had a larger plan: "[Eve's] offspring shall bruise [the serpent's] head."[71] Out of the blessed creation would come the Blessed One who would destroy the evil one and remove forever the curse of damnation. Even in the fall, God determined to bless. What had been meant for evil, God intended for good[72]: He would bring life out of death,[73] victory out of defeat,[74] blessing out of curse.[75] God himself would be a path of repentance and return (*teshuvah*) for fallen man. His provision would draw man to himself in a relationship of pure love, voluntarily given from a free will.

COVENANT AND BLESSING

All accurate teaching on theology and anthropology, then, must begin with covenant and blessing, not with fall and redemption. God is a God of covenant and blessing. He makes covenant with those whom he draws near to himself in faith. Indeed, God has always sought men and women who would be joined in covenant with him and receive his benediction as a result. God's will is that all men be saved; therefore, he has made provision in Christ's passion to atone for the sins of the entire human race.

Even after the fall, God demonstrated his ongoing covenant with mankind by sacrificing an animal to provide a covering for sin.[76] The clothing that covered Adam and Eve's nakedness was a symbol to remind them of their rebellion against God. This is clearly demonstrated in the fact that the Hebrew word for clothing (*beged*) is virtually the same as that for rebellion (*begad*). It is also a demonstration that God's covenant with mankind was not completely severed but now became contingent upon the future sacrifice of the Lamb slain from the foundation of the world. Likewise, mankind's dominion over the earth was not completely revoked despite the fact that their act of rebellion sold them into slavery to the serpent. Again, the dominion was to be fully restored by the one who would reclaim the keys from Satan[77] following his own sinless, victorious life in the same flesh in which Adam had failed.[78]

In all of history since the creation, God has repeatedly entered into covenant with those who have drawn near to him, and as a result of his covenantal relationship, he has blessed them. Blessing has not been some unusual, occasional divine quirk. God's ongoing blessing has always been an outworking of his nature. As love personified, he must manifest love in the truest sense of the Hebraic emphasis on verbs, not nouns. God is not love in some static, substantive sense. He is love in an active, demonstrative sense. God is love because God loves.

The first outworking of love is blessing, the desire to bring good to the objects of one's love. Love is not something that is, it is something that one does. If earthly parents are driven to bless their children by their good deeds, how much more does the Heavenly Father desire to bring blessing into the lives of his children?[79] Blessing, then, is an essential part of the divine economy. "It has a definite beginning, cannot be disannuled by man, [and] is visible and abounding. God challenges men to secure it,"[80] says S. Maxwell Coder, dean of education emeritus at Moody Bible Institute. God will not rest until he has fully blessed his creation by restoring the Garden of Eden experience of face-to-face relationship, with man living in the very presence of God, basking in the pristine light of his glory and blessing.[81]

[1] Romans 3:23; 5:12.
[2] Psalm 51:5, TNK.
[3] Romans 7:19, KJV.
[4] Romans 3:10.
[5] Romans 8:3; 7:24-25.
[6] 1 Timothy 3:16.
[7] Hebrews 4:15.
[8] Hebrews 2:14; Revelation 1:18.
[9] 2 Corinthians 5:20.
[10] John 1:29.

[11] Renner, " 'Believing' in the Beginning of Blessing-History," p. 50.

[12] John 9:3.

[13] Augustine, *Contra Julius*, II, X, 33.

[14] With this idea, Origen's thought was foundational to the doctrine of ultimate reconciliation of universalist theology.

[15] 4 Esdras 3:21-22; 4:30.

[16] Louis Berkhof, *Systematic Theology* (Grand Rapids: Wm. B. Eerdmans, 1996), p. 251.

[17] Romans 8:3; Hebrews 2:14.

[18] Albert Henry Newman, *Manual of Church History*, Vol. 1 (1986), p. 366.

[19] Romans 6:1.

[20] Revelation 22:17.

[21] From the web site *www.ccel.org/a/arminius/works3/html*.

[22] S. Schechter, *Some Aspects of Rabbinic Theology* (New York: The Macmillan Company, 1910), pp. 242-263.

[23] Genesis 8:21.

[24] W.O.E. Oesterly, *The Religion and Worship of the Synagogue* (New York: Charles Scribner's Sons, 1907), pp. 242-243.

[25] The idea that the *yetzer hatov* is manifest at the age of thirteen is based on *Midrash Kohelet* 9:14. It is the likely origin for the emergence in the last two centuries of the practice of *bar mitzvah* (son of the commandment), at which boys accept the Torah and assume responsibility for their own actions.

[26] Romans 7:19-21.

[27] 2 Corinthians 10:5, ASV.

[28] Genesis 1:26-27; 5:1-3.

[29] Genesis 2:7.

[30] 2 Timothy 3:16.

[31] Romans 3:2, NIV.

[32] Romans 2:15.

[33] Job 32:8.

[34] Psalm 119:105.

[35] Romans 10:17.

[36] Renner, " 'Believing' in the Beginning of Blessing-History," p. 49.

[37] Psalm 51:5, KJV.

[38] Psalm 119:73.

[39] Psalm 100:3.

[40] Zechariah 12:1.

[41] Jeremiah 1:5; Galatians 1:15.

[42] 1 Corinthians 11:7.

[43] James 3:9.

[44] William Cheshire, M.D., "He Knoweth the Secrets of the Heart" *Restore!* Issue 4.

[45] Deuteronomy 11:20.

[46] Jeremiah 17:9.

[47] Proverbs 20:27.

[48] Luke 24:13-32.

[49] Luke 24:45, NIV.

[50] The idea of the divine conjunction of mind, heart, and the Word of God has been expounded brilliantly by my friend and colleague, Dr. Karl D. Coke, and is the source of this exposition.

[51] 1 Timothy 4:2; Romans 1:28; 2 Thessalonians 2:11.

[52] Genesis 1:22, 28.

[53] Genesis 5:2.

[54] Genesis 1:26, 28.

[55] Galatians 3:8.

[56] Hebrews 4:2-4.

[57] Daniel 7:18, 27.

[58] Luke 22:30.

[59] Matthew 25:34.

[60] Revelation 20:6.

[61] Habakkuk 2:14.

[62] Genesis 3:22.

[63] Jude 1:6.

[64] John 21:20.

[65] 1 John 4:8,16.

[66] 1 John 4:10.

[67] John 3:16-17.

[68] Genesis 3:14.

[69] Genesis 3:17.

[70] Genesis 3:16, 19.

[71] Genesis 3:15.

[72] Genesis 50:20.

[73] Romans 5:17.

[74] Isaiah 25:8; 1 Corinthians 15:54.

[75] Revelation 22:3.

[76] Genesis 3:21.

[77] Revelation 1:18.

[78] Romans 5:12, 17.

[79] Matthew 7:11.

[80] S. Maxwell Coder, in William Evans, *The Great Doctrines of the Bible* (Chicago: Moody Press, 1974), p. 280.

[81] Revelation 21:23.

Chapter 3

God's Personal Blessing

The most profound blessing in all of Holy Scripture is the one that God himself composed. What is more important, though, is that God established a system by which this blessing would be placed upon his children and he gave a solemn command that his plan be fulfilled in each generation so that all believers in the one God would be blessed with the Creator's own personal benediction. This blessing might even be called, "The Blessing."

Even though it is often referred to as the Aaronic benediction because of the directive making the sons of Aaron responsible for placing the blessing upon the children of Israel, "The Blessing" is God's blessing. The Eternal even dictated the exact language of this benediction to Moses: "The LORD bless thee, and keep thee: The LORD make his face shine upon thee, and be gracious unto thee: The LORD lift up his countenance upon thee, and give thee peace."[1] In the Hebrew Scriptures, the blessing reads:[2]

יְבָרֶכְךָ ה' וְיִשְׁמְרֶךָ

יָאֵר ה' פָּנָיו אֵלֶיךָ וִיחֻנֶּךָ

יִשָּׂא ה' פָּנָיו אֵלֶיךָ וְיָשֵׂם לְךָ שָׁלוֹם

In Christian circles, this most beautiful and powerful of all biblical benedictions is repeated occasionally by a liturgist or minister, usually at the conclusion of a worship service or some other spiritual exercise. It is often believed that one must be part of the ordained clergy in order to be vested with the authority to give this blessing. For most Christians, it is likely little more than a signal that the minister has finally concluded his sermon and that they have reached the end of the worship service. The powerful import of the blessing is, therefore, often obscured.

In the Jewish community, the blessing that was pronounced by Aaron's sons in the temple is now spoken by the descendants of those ancient priests during the present-day synagogue liturgy. More importantly, however, in observant Jewish homes it is placed upon children by their parents. This interesting Jewish use of the blessing is taken from the specific words of Scripture that require these words to be said over "children of Israel." Since the Jewish home is viewed as a sanctuary parallel with the Jerusalem temple, parents take the responsibility of blessing their children in their homes.

Why is this blessing so powerful in evoking images of God's hand extended to overshadow the worshiper and impact his own blessing by giving his children peace? Perhaps it has such great consequences for believers because it reflects the personality and mission of God himself in relationship to his people.

A TRIPARTITE BLESSING

"The Blessing" is in reality three blessings in one. When the Scriptures were divided into chapters and verses, three verses were assigned to this one blessing, one verse for each statement in the blessing. The blessing is three complete sentences. It could have read, "The Lord bless and keep you, make his face to shine upon you, lift up his countenance upon you, and give you peace." In fact, however, each of the three blessings invokes the personal name of God, ה/ו/ה/י (Y/H/W/H, Yah/weh),[3] the name that God chose for himself to reveal himself to humanity.[4]

The name of God reveals his character. Since it essentially means in Hebrew, "I am that I am," or "I will be what I will be," or "I will be [there]," it is a statement by God of his own eternity. There has never been a time when he was not, and there will never be a time when he will not be. Indeed, he dwells outside time in the eternal present. He simply is! The name is also a statement of God's aseity, for he alone in the universe is the source of his own existence. "I am because I am," his name declares. Everything else exists because God created it. God, however, is simply because he is.

The fact that God stamped his personal name on each of the three blessings within "The Blessing" is evidence that each of the three statements is equally from God and bears equal weight. The three blessings reveal something about the very nature and mission of God in relationship to the creation that is being blessed. There is only one blessing; however, it is a tripartite benediction.

Fundamental to the understanding of God is the concept of monotheism. There is only one God. The Jewish people assert that God is absolutely one and that no possibility of plurality exists in him. He is forever incorporeal. The most common Christian understanding of the nature of God is that there is only one God, one being of substance, who is manifest in three persons. The divine substance is spirit, for "God is Spirit."[5] The three persons are the Father, the Son, and the Holy Spirit.[6] The fact that these three are one is the divine mystery of deity.[7] Though some have asserted that this way of describing God is based in ancient mystery religions, the truth is that it is solidly rooted in the Hebrew Scriptures themselves, including the Apostolic Scriptures. It also has foundations in the speculation of Jewish sages that likely preceded the Christian era and found formulation in the writings of medieval Jewish philosophers who viewed God as King (crown), Word, and *Shekhinah* (spirit).[8]

Since there are three persons in God, it is perfectly appropriate that there are three blessings in "The Blessing" and that the three blessings together comprise the one blessing. It might be suggested, therefore, that the first blessing is from the Father, the second is from the Son, and the third is from the Holy Spirit.

The first blessing in the tripartite benediction states, "The Lord bless you and keep you." This blessing from the heavenly Father reveals two things about God's nature as Father that are manifest in the nature of fatherhood wherever it appears. It is essential to the character of fatherhood to bless and to keep. The Father in heaven is one who has an unrelenting determination to bless his creation and to keep them. He has made every sacrifice possible to provide for man's blessing, and he is the one who guards and protects his children. David noted this truth: "The Lord is my shepherd, I shall not want."[9] Interestingly enough, the Father's blessing in Hebrew is exactly three words, יְבָרֶכְךָ ה' וְיִשְׁמְרֶךָ, which is the number associated with the Divine.

The blessing of the Son declares, "The Lord shine his face upon you and be gracious to you." This blessing comes from the person of the Word, the Son of God. It is the Son's unique function to reveal the Father, to put a face on him, as it were. The Eternal Father is ineffable, inscrutable, unknown, and unrevealed. He has never been seen–nor can he be seen–by any human being, for he dwells in light which no man can approach.[10] What is known of the Father is what he has chosen to reveal through the person of the Word, his Son. John observed this powerful truth: "No one has seen God at any time. The only begotten son . . . has declared him."[11] In him was light and the light was the light of men.

The person of God who caused God's face to shine upon mankind was the Son. The Scriptures say that "the Son is the radiance of God's glory and the exact representation of his being."[12] God has caused his glory to shine in the face of Jesus Christ.[13] It is also true that grace and truth uniquely came through Jesus Christ.[14] Indeed, Jesus is the personification of God's grace. Interestingly enough, the blessing of the Son in Hebrew is exactly five words, יָאֵר ה' פָּנָיו אֵלֶיךָ וִיחֻנֶּךָּ, the biblical number that is often associated with grace.

The blessing of the Holy Spirit reads: "The Lord turn his face toward you and give you peace." The Holy Spirit is the person of God who proceeds from the Father and the Son and engages the hearts of believers. His prevenient grace confronts man with the face of God and woos him into relationship with the Divine.

The Holy Spirit is also the agent of God's peace. The Hebrew word for peace is the very familiar *shalom*. The import of this part of the Holy Spirit's blessing is profound, for it speaks not so much of peace as of wholeness, health, restoration, and the absence of conflict. The Holy Spirit is the agent of God's peace, for he is the channel of God's love. The love of God is poured out into believers' hearts by the Holy Spirit.[15] The Holy Spirit produces the fruits of the Spirit that include peace in a sequence that begins from love and flows through joy into peace.[16] It is also interesting that the blessing of the Holy Spirit in Hebrew is exactly seven words, יִשָּׂא ה' פָּנָיו אֵלֶיךָ וְיָשֵׂם לְךָ שָׁלוֹם, corresponding to the seven spirits of God through which the Holy Spirit flows.[17] The Holy Spirit is associated with this number of perfection that is seen in the menorah (seven-branched lampstand), in the days of the week, and in the notes of the musical scale.

The ultimate result of "The Blessing" is the manifestation of peace, the benediction's final word. God's final word for humanity is, "*Shalom*" ("Peace"). Blessing is, therefore, God's ultimate intention for mankind. It is sin in the world that produces conflict and turmoil. The presence of the Holy Spirit brings peace, for there is no condemnation to those who walk in the Spirit.[18] They have peace with God. In the Spirit they do not fulfill the desires of the flesh; therefore, they are removed from the sin that causes alienation from God and the conflict that it produces.

THE LITURGY OF BLESSING

The divine blessing was first spoken over the congregation of Israel by the sons of Aaron in the tabernacle. Later it was spoken over worshipers in the temple. Until the time of Christ, the priests distinctly uttered the Divine Name (*Y/H/W/H*) in pronouncing the blessing because God himself declared that the blessing would affix his name on the blessed. After the death of Simon the Just, some forty years before the destruction of the temple in 70 A.D., this practice was discontinued, and the word *Adonai* was substituted for the divine name.

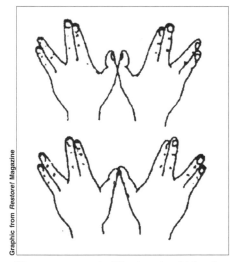

Graphic from *Restore!* Magazine

The arrangement of the hands of blessing by the priests of Israel so that the *Shekhinah* glory passed through their fingers and blessed the chosen people of God.

In the liturgy of the temple, the three portions of the benediction were pronounced without pause, after which the people responded, "Blessed be the Lord God, the God of Israel from eternity to eternity." Elsewhere, the priests paused after each sentence, and the people responded, "Amen." Additionally, the priests were required to remove their leather footwear when they ascended to give the blessing, and they were to stand facing the congregation out of respect for the people as they spoke the words of benediction.

The priests always gave the blessing with their hands uplifted. It was believed that when they did so, the *Shekhinah* hovered over their heads and its rays gleamed through their open fingers. To this day when the *Cohanim* (descendants of the ancient priests) pronounce the blessing, they raise their hands with the thumb and first finger and the middle and ring fingers separated so that the rays of the *Shekhinah* may pass through to those being blessed. The people were not permitted to look upon the priests while the blessing was being said. This gave rise to the practice that those who are being blessed cover their heads with a *tallith* (prayer shawl) during the benediction.

The blessing had no magical powers. It was God, not the priests, who blessed: "I will bless them," God said. These specific words were used so that the Israelites could not say that their well-being depended upon the priests' blessings. The Jewish people always understood that God alone can bless.

A PERPETUAL COMMAND TO BLESS

The divine blessing is not a mere ceremonial formality, nor is it optional. It is God's command that his children be blessed in perpetuity with the benediction that he formulated. This threefold blessing is powerful and perpetual. It is the generationally enduring promise of divine favor and all that it provides. It is a very personal blessing for the lowliest of humans from the exalted Sovereign of the universe.

---

[1] Numbers 6:24-26, KJV.

[2] Out of deference to our Jewish friends' sensitivity for the use of the Tetragrammaton in a work such as this, we have substituted 'ה for ה/ו/ה/י in this Hebrew citation of the blessing. (See footnote 3.)

³ We have included slashes between the letters of the Tetragrammaton out of respect for Jewish conviction that writing the name or attempting to pronounce it is disrespectful to God. In Jewish tradition, the Ineffable Name is written only on Torah scrolls and in *Siddurim* which are carefully protected because they contain the Divine Name. Any book or scroll in which the Tetragrammaton is written may never be discarded or burned. It must, rather, be buried.

⁴ This name is called the Ineffable Name by the Jewish people because it is never pronounced. Because of their care not to violate the third of the Ten Commandments ("You shall not take the name of the Lord your God in vain."), the Jewish people since before the time of Jesus have substituted the word *Adonai* (Lord) for the name *Yah/weh* in their reading of the Scriptures and in their reciting of "The Blessing" and other benedictions. The Masoretic text of the Hebrew Scriptures uses the vowel points of the name *Elohim* as the vowel points for the name *Yah/weh* so that *Adonai* will be read as a substitute for *Yah/weh*.

⁵ John 4:24.

⁶ The persons of God are understood by some in the context of the Latin *persona*, which is more accurately rendered "role." Others have suggested modalistic manifestations of God. Still others have suggested that the Father alone is God. These and other ideas have produced massive and generationally enduring debate in which varying shades of interpretation have been offered, including hair-splitting over minutiae. The orthodox understanding of God, the doctrine of the Trinity, is a clear statement of monotheism and is supported both by Holy Scripture and by ideas from many Jewish traditions.

⁷ 1 Timothy 3:16.

⁸ See Rabbi Tzvi Nassi (Hirsch Prinz), *The Great Mystery or How Can Three Be One?* (Cincinnati: M.L.O.).

⁹ Psalm 23:1.

¹⁰ 1 Timothy 6:16.

¹¹ John 1:18.

¹² Hebrews 1:3, NIV.

¹³ 2 Corinthians 4:6.

¹⁴ John 1:17.

¹⁵ Romans 5:5.

¹⁶ Galatians 5:22.

¹⁷ Revelation 4:5.

¹⁸ Romans 8:1.

Chapter 4

Applying the Divine Name

The perpetual requirement that the tripartite divine blessing be spoken over the children of God in each generation also ensured that the Divine Name would be placed on each of God's children. The implications of this are profound and far-reaching and have amazing consequences for those who are so blessed. The blessing command that specifies the words that are to be spoken over God's children concludes with this statement: "They shall put my name upon the children of Israel, and I will bless them." The act of blessing the covenantal people affixes the Divine Name upon those who are blessed. A spiritual act transfers God's own personal name to those who receive his benediction.

Originally, the Jewish people pronounced the Divine Name, ה/ו/ה/י (*Y/H/W/H, Yah/weh*), with every greeting and blessing so as to make it efficacious.[1] Later, it became the privilege of the priests to use the name in blessing the people. Because God had declared that when the priests blessed the people they placed God's name on them, the reverential sanctity that came to be attached to the name gave the priestly function a mystical power.

In its earliest application, the priestly blessing involved two acts. First, the words of the benediction were spoken. Then, the Divine Name was written by the priest either in the hand or on the forehead of the worshiper.[2] Later, it came to be understood that the words of the blessing affixed the Divine Name because the blessing was given in the name itself, thrice repeated. Because the blessing applied the Divine Name to the blessed, some have observed that the third commandment ("You shall not take the name of the Lord your God in vain.") demanded that those who bore the Divine Name in their foreheads should not misbehave, for if they were to do so, they would desecrate that Name.[3]

The precision of fulfillment of this profound promise was of such import to ancient Israel that, even when Israelite leaders ceased from using the Divine Name in ordinary discourse and in general worship exercises for fear of violating the Decalogue's third commandment, the priests of Israel continued to employ the Divine Name in the divine blessing. Eventually, even this practice ceased so that for some time the Divine Name was used only by the High Priest and finally only on the Day of Atonement and then in such hushed tones that it was lost in the liturgical chanting. Ultimately, even this limited use was discontinued, and the Divine Name was never spoken. Jewish people to this day refer to God as *Adonai* (Lord) or simply as *haShem* (the Name), and they consider any attempt to enunciate the Divine Name as blasphemy.

Even though the intention of the Israelites in first limiting and then eliminating the use of the spoken Divine Name was based in the piety of respect for the Eternal and the fear of somehow dishonoring him, the fact remains that God himself composed and dictated the Divine Blessing and declared that when it was spoken over his children, it resulted in his name's being written on those who are blessed.

COVENANT, BLESSING, AND GOD'S NAME

The single most powerful example of God's covenant with man, the consequent blessing, and the resultant application of the Divine Name occurred in the lives of Abraham and Sarah, the progenitors of the faith race. They first came into covenant relationship with God when they left their own country and people and followed God's direction to the Promised Land. Then, they were given the blessing of the Eternal upon their lives and the lives of their progeny. As a direct result of this covenant and blessing, they both experienced a name change in which the Divine Name was added to their birth names.

Abraham's name at birth was אַבְרָם (Avram or Abram). Apparently his parents had high expectations for him because the name they chose for him meant "exalted father." In ancient times, names were not chosen solely for their sound or impression but as expressions of expectations about the character or destiny of the infant. Avram's family, therefore, envisioned greatness in their son when they named him "Exalted Father." It must have seemed quite ironic that one whose name was Exalted Father should have had no children when he was more than eighty years old. Indeed, Avram despaired of ever having children, thinking that his fortune would be inherited by his steward. Even when God promised that he and his wife would have a son, Avram laughed at such an unlikely prospect.

Sarah's birth name was שָׂרַי (Sarai), which meant "my princess" and could be interpreted as meaning "a controlling woman."[4] She, too, had laughed at God's promise that she, an octogenarian, would give birth to a son. Indeed, when she first heard the promise, she devised a plan by which she could assist God in bringing forth what for her was impossible. As a "controlling woman" she was attempting to manipulate her environment when she enlisted Hagar as a surrogate mother to bear Avram's son. The result was problematic for both Avram and Sarai, and it has remained a root of contention ever since that time. Ishmael and his descendants have continued to be a source of conflict for Avram's progeny through Isaac even to the present day.

IMPLEMENTING THE COVENANT AND BLESSING

When the time came for God's relationship with Avram and Sarai to reach full flower, the circumstances could not have been more daunting. Avram was 99 years of age, and Sarai was 90. The writer of Hebrews notes that Avram was "as good as dead," and Sarai was at least 40 years postmenopausal. It was, indeed, a laughing matter that they together could produce a son to fulfill the promise. Both Avram and Sarai chuckled at the prospect, and perhaps Sarai more than Avram, for the idea was even more challengingly impossible for her than for her husband. She would have to carry the promised child in her elderly womb for nine months!

It was at this time that God appeared to Avram and confirmed his covenant with him: "I will establish my covenant as an everlasting covenant between me and you and your descendants after you for the generations to come, to be your God and the God of your descendants after you. . . . Your wife Sarah will bear you a son, and you will call him Isaac. I will establish my covenant with him as an everlasting covenant for his descendants after him. . . . My covenant I will establish with Isaac, whom Sarah shall bear to you at this set time next year."[5] Not only did God promise Avram that his descendants would be numerous, he also was very specific in even naming the immediate channel of fulfillment and predicting precisely the time of his birth. The Abrahamic covenant would be established in Isaac whom the ninety-year-old Sarai would birth. It is a bit of divine irony that the name which God assigned to the child יִצְחָק (*Yitzhak*, Isaac) literally meant "laughter," which was both Avram and Sarai's initial response to God's impossible promise.

During this confirmation of the Abrahamic covenant,

something profound and mystical occurred. God changed both Avram and Sarai's names, renaming them more appropriately to describe their new roles as covenant partners with God. This was in perfect order with the ancient Eastern custom of exchanging names or parts of names when parties entered into a covenantal relationship. Interestingly enough, this millennia-old custom is still manifest in the covenant of marriage, when either the bride receives the name of the groom or, in some cases, both names are exchanged so that both husband and wife afterward bear one another's family names.

Since the Abrahamic covenant was a unilateral covenant, only Abraham and Sarah's names were changed. They both received a part of the Divine Name that was implanted in their birth names to give them new meaning, demonstrating their change of status for having joined with God in the covenant of blessing.

UNDERSTANDING THE DIVINE NAME

God's personal name is ה/ו/ה/י (*Y/H/W/H, Yah/weh*).[6] This name is called the Tetragrammaton, which is Greek for "four letters." In reality, however, there are only three letters in the Divine Name, י (*yod*), ו (*vav*), and ה (*heh*), with the ה (*heh*) repeated twice. Interestingly enough, the Divine Name is composed of three and only three Hebrew letters.

Since nothing that God does is by happenstance, it should come as no surprise that the name he chose for himself has profound significance, not only in its meaning, but also in its very composition. The three letters of the Divine Name represent the three persons manifest in the one God, the one being of substance. These three are the Father, the Son, and the Holy Spirit.

The י (*yod*) in the Divine Name may be understood to represent the Father.[7] It is interesting that the *yod* is the only letter in the Hebrew alphabet that never descends to the bottom line. It remains at the top line. So it is with the Heavenly Father, who never descends to be seen of men. He dwells in the heaven of heavens, wholly inaccessible to mankind.

In the Hebrew language, each letter of the alphabet (or *aleph-beth*, the origin of the term) is a pictograph, a vivid portrayal of a common object in the lives of the ancient people. For example, the first letter, *aleph*, was originally a symbol for an ox head and the second letter, *beth*, was a picture of a house. The letter *yod* represents a hand. That this symbol should be representative of the Eternal Father in the Divine Name can be understood in that the hand symbolizes power and control. It is the Father who is the ultimate seat of power and controls and moves all things to his designed purposes.

The ו (*vav*) in the Divine Name may be understood to represent the Son, the person of God whose function is to reveal the Father.[8] The Son is the person of the Word,[9] the truth of God[10] who enlightens all men and brings them to salvation and relationship with God. It is certainly interesting that the *vav* is nothing more than a *yod* that has been extended to the bottom line. It was the person of the Son of God who fully manifest the essence of the Father in heaven before men on earth.[11] He personally became incarnate so he could reveal the Father. "If you have seen me, you have seen the Father," he declared.[12]

The pictograph of the letter ו (*vav*) is a nail. What better alphabetic semaphore could be used to signify the immeasurable impact of the Son of God upon humanity than the very nail that affixed Jesus to the cross and thereby fully demonstrated God's unfathomable love for humanity? The suffering and death of the Son was the fullest manifestation of the divine being who is perfect love. The mystery is that in order to secure the fulfillment of his eternal determination of covenant and blessing for humankind, God gave himself as the Lamb[13] to atone for all sin and restore man's relationship with the Creator. He gave himself in the person of his Son who extended the Father to the bottom line and fully revealed the Father as man's lover, not his judge, by allowing the nails of Calvary to penetrate his flesh and release the blood of atonement.

The ה (*heh*) in the Divine Name may be understood to represent the Holy Spirit. It is used twice because the Holy Spirit proceeds both from the Father and the Son. Indeed the Divine Name is composed of *yod/heh* and *vav/heh*, and in that order. The ה (*heh*) is the breath sound in Hebrew and in its transliterations. Pronunciation of the letter ה (*heh*) as with the letter *h* in English requires the exhalation of breath. One needs only to exhale to speak this part of the Divine Name.

It is no coincidence, then, that this letter represents the Holy Spirit, for the Hebrew word for spirit (*ruach*) means spirit, air, and wind. This is why Jesus' use of the metaphor of wind to describe the Holy Spirit and his function was so graphic for his Jewish audience.[14] It is also interesting to note that the action that vivified the body of the first human being was the infusion of the divine breath. When God breathed into Adam's nostrils the breath of life, he became a living soul.[15] Likewise, when Jesus prepared his disciples for the calvary experience, he "breathed on them and said, 'Receive you the Holy Spirit.' "[16]

The Holy Spirit is the person of God who goes beyond the Son's role in revealing the Father and brings the Father into personal contact with mankind. He is the person who enables human beings to experience God. He imbues humankind with the divine presence. When the Holy Spirit is present, what is impossible for men becomes routine with God.

The ה (*heh*) is also a pictograph of a window. In the very structure of the letter itself one can see a window. It is the Holy Spirit that is man's window into the heavenlies. Those who viewed scenes of divine awe were "in the Spirit" when they experienced the apocalyptic.[17] It is the Holy Spirit who is the agent for imparting God's blessings: "I will open the windows of heaven and pour you out a blessing."[18]

THE COVENANTAL NAME CHANGE

Avram and Sarai's covenant with God necessitated a name change. In their case, the unilateral divine covenant required only that their names be changed by adding a part of God's name to their birth names. And so it was. The ה (*heh*) from the divine name was implanted into both Abram and Sarai. אַבְרָם (*Avram*) became אַבְרָהָם (*Avraham*), and שָׂרַי (*Sarai*) became שָׂרָה (*Sarah*).

The change of names by the infusion of part of God's name brought a change of status and ability. The name changes reflected the infusion of the divine presence into the lives of both Abraham and Sarah. The Holy Spirit (the breath of God) was imbued into their geriatric lives, imparting to them youthful vigor and making the impossible not only possible but practical.

What was impossible before now became expected. Abraham was no longer "exalted father." He became the "father of many nations" (the meaning of his new name). When Abraham was vivified by the Holy Spirit, he no longer focused on personal concerns. He became the blesser of all the nations of the world.

Sarah no longer was a "controlling woman," she became a "princess with God." When she received the Holy Spirit, she no longer tried to control their lives and effect the divine promise by human means. As "God's princess," she surrendered her control to the Holy Spirit so that the impossible could occur in her life, much as it would centuries later in the life of Mary who experienced an even more miraculous birth when she said to God and his angel: "Be it unto me according to thy word."[19]

The very names that God gave to Abraham and Sarah, then, reflected the true nature of fulfillment for his promise and blessing. It was not through their own human strength that the generational blessing was to be fulfilled. It was through the agency of the Holy Spirit, the motive force of all creation that the miracle would occur. The ה (*heh*) or "h" factor powerfully impacted both of their lives and produced an impossible blessing that was the fountainhead of all future blessings: the son of promise was born.

REALIZING THE BLESSING

With the entrance of the Holy Spirit into Abraham and Sarah's lives, the blessing was fulfilled the next year, just as God had promised. Isaac ("laughter") was born. When the Holy Spirit is present, promises that have seemed long forgotten and unfulfilled suddenly spring to life. The blessing is realized. Through the agency of the Holy Spirit, God summons into reality things that are not[20] just as he did in the days of primeval genesis when he created everything that exists *ex nihilo* (out of nothing).

The Creator is still creating as the Holy Spirit is still moving upon the face of the waters of humanity.[21] God's creative force has not been abated, nor has it been restricted by men's assertion that he no longer does things like those in the biblical record. The Eternal never changes.[22] With God, there is neither variableness nor shadow of turning.[23] Jesus Christ is the same yesterday, and today, and forever.[24] The Holy Spirit remains the irresistible force and ever generates miracles in the lives of those who believe and receive his empowerment. The covenant and the blessing survive and are made sure to men and women of faith.

"Nothing is impossible with God," Jesus declared.[25] "I can do all things through Christ who strengthens me," Paul exclaimed.[26] Jesus promised, "Whatever you ask for in prayer, believe that you have received it, and it will be yours."[27] And, therein is the secret of receiving the blessing. One must believe that he has received it when he asks, and it will be done.

These ideas of receiving the promised blessing were not new to Jesus or Paul, however. David declared it: "Take delight in the Lord, and he will give you the desires of your heart."[28] The Psalmist observed that delighting in the Lord is synonymous with delighting in his Word and instruction (commandments).[29] John the apostle confirmed the formula for receiving the blessing: "[We] receive from him anything we ask, because we obey his commands and do what pleases him."[30]

Receiving the blessing is not based on acquiring the knowledge of secret formulae or cryptic incantations or even mindless repetition of spiritual mantras. Blessing from God is realized in exactly the same manner in which Abraham's hopes were fulfilled. Believe and practice the Word of God, delighting to do God's bidding. Get up and go in the walk of faith. Trust God, and await the infusion of the Holy Spirit's creative power. The God of covenant will fulfill his Word and bring blessing.

THE BLESSING AND THE NAME FOR BELIEVERS

What was true of Abraham is true for all believers. Abraham is the father of all who have faith in the same God that the patriarch worshiped. When the Holy Spirit enters a believer's life, he becomes a new creation[31] and a part of Abraham's family.[32] Like Abraham, believers who come to faith have crossed over, being translated out of the kingdom of darkness into the kingdom of God's dear Son.[33] As such, they also have become Hebrews. Because they belong to the Messiah, they are both "Abraham's children and heirs according to the promise."[34]

The new covenant confirmed through the death and resurrection of the Messiah is but a renewal of that most ancient of covenants, God's covenant with Abraham. Its basis is the same as that of the archetypal covenant: faith.[35]

The covenant is renewed each time someone chooses to exercise his human will to believe what God has said and accept the divine atonement for sin. The word of the good news that has penetrated a darkened heart generates faith that is then released to God. God, in turn, accepts man's faith and credits the righteousness of Christ in its stead.[36] Just as Abraham was saved from his Babylonian milieu solely by his faith in the Divine which prompted him to begin the walk of faith that brought him to the Promised Land, so the pagan heart is renewed by the same faith to begin a walk of confidence on the narrow path that leads to the narrow gate of everlasting life.[37]

Beyond their inheritance of the Abrahamic covenant, believers also receive the divine blessing that God placed on Abraham. They are added to the number of the children of Abraham who are eternally blessed of God. They are entitled to the personal blessing that God composed and ordered to be placed on his children by his priests. They legitimately receive "The Blessing," and because they also become a part of the priesthood of all believers,[38] they also receive the right to pronounce that benediction upon the children of God.

In addition to being entitled to the blessing and its benefits, believers also receive the impartation of the Divine Name. Is it any wonder, then, that in John's apocalyptic vision, the redeemed children of Abraham have the Father's name written in their foreheads?[39] The same name that was placed upon Abraham when he entered into covenant with God and received the divine blessing is also placed upon those who through the Messiah have become the children of God. The same name that was placed upon the Israelites by the Aaronic priests when the divine blessing was spoken over them is also placed upon Christians who come to faith in God.

The Christian name change, however, is not a literal renaming. It is the Holy Spirit that is imbued into their

lives that inscribes God's name on their hearts and in their
minds. God is not fixated with the external surface of the
human cranium, hoping to stamp some indelible brand
upon it. He is concerned that the human mind be infused
with the divine mind through the Holy Spirit so that the
Lawgiver himself writes his divine instructions on one's
heart and mind. This is the essence of the new covenant of
divine grace: "I will write my laws in their minds and in
their hearts."[40] It is the Holy Spirit who inscribes the divine law on man's heart. And, it is the Holy Spirit who
effects the nomenclature change of human definition from
sinner to saint, from unbeliever to Christian, from heathen
to child of Abraham, from Gentile to Israelite.

The four-millennia-old covenant of Abraham, then,
includes all his children, both linear descendants and spiritual descendants through the Messiah. Likewise, the blessing that began in one man's faithfulness is extended to all
men of faith. Accordingly, the imprint of the Divine Name
is indelibly made upon the minds of those who choose to
believe and obey. They bear the name of their Father in
heaven as they manifest the works and character of their
earthly father, Abraham.

[1] "The Priestly Blessing," *JewishEncyclopedia.com*, p. 4.
[2] Meir Bar-Ilan, "They Shall Put My Name upon the People of
Israel," *Hebrew Union College Annual Journal* 60 (1989), pp. 19-31.
[3] *Ibid.*
[4] This is Strong's definition.
[5] Genesis 17:7, 19 (NIV), 21.
[6] See note 3 on page 56.
[7] 1 Timothy 6:16; John 6:46.
[8] John 1:18.
[9] John 1:1-4.
[10] John 14:6.
[11] Colossians 2:9.
[12] John 14:9.
[13] John 1:29, 36.
[14] John 3:8.
[15] Genesis 2:7.
[16] John 20:22.

[17] 1 Samuel 16:13; Ezekiel 3:14; Luke 4:14; Revelation 1:10.
[18] Malachi 3:10.
[19] Luke 1:38.
[20] Romans 4:17.
[21] Genesis 1:2.
[22] Malachi 3:6.
[23] James 1:17.
[24] Hebrews 13:8.
[25] Luke 1:37.
[26] Philippians 4:13.
[27] Mark 11:24, NIV.
[28] Psalm 37:4, RSV.
[29] Psalm 40:8.
[30] 1 John 3:22.
[31] 2 Corinthians 5:17.
[32] Romans 4:16.
[33] Colossians 1:13.
[34] Galatians 3:29.
[35] Romans 5:1.
[36] Romans 4:22.
[37] Matthew 7:14.
[38] Revelation 1:6.
[39] Revelation 14:1; 22:4.
[40] Jeremiah 31:33; Hebrews 10:16.

Chapter 5

The Blessing Continuum

The Abrahamic covenant, with its attendant blessing, was not made solely for Abraham's benefit. It was a blessing to bless. Abraham was blessed so that he might also be a blessing to all nations, to all the families of the earth. God's blessing is never designed solely for the benefit of the one who is divinely blessed. It is always a blessing to bless. God's blessing initiates a chain reaction of blessings. The one who is blessed is expected to be a channel through which the blessing can flow into the lives of others. Ultimately, the blessing returns to God who gave it. When God's blessed people–whether direct recipients of his blessing or indirect beneficiaries of his blessing through others–offer their thanks to God for his beneficence, the act of thanksgiving completes the circle of blessing.

BLESSING AND GRACE

The source of all blessing is God himself, and the means by which blessing is conveyed is divine grace. The blessing of God is never merited by man. Nothing that men can do–even punctilious performance of divine commands–is adequate to merit God's favor. Divine grace is simply an outpouring of the essence of Divine Personality: love. God's love so transcends the upper limits of man's capacity for love that man's love appears infinitesimal by comparison. The secret of the infinite divine love is that God *is* love. God's determination to love, therefore, is unrelenting and can never be abandoned. He is ever searching for those on whom he can lavish his love. The outworking of God's love is his unmerited favor, the grace that he extends to his children.

In the Apostolic Scriptures the word for grace is χάρις (*charis*), which means "charm, good will, or favor." This word directly corresponds to the Hebrew word חֵן (*chen*) which means "favor, grace, charm, elegance, or acceptance." The context of χάρις in the new covenant, however, also implies loving kindness, which is best described in the Hebrew Scriptures by the word חֶסֶד (*chesed*). *Chesed* means "goodness, kindness, or faithfulness." When it speaks of God's *chesed*, however, the word is almost indefinable, for it speaks of God's loving kindness, his mercy that is boundless and unfathomable. *Chesed* is parallel with רָחַם (*racham*), which means "mercy." This word is the root of the word רֶחֶם *rechem*, which means "womb." These words portray a poignant picture of God's grace as parallel with the safest environment for a totally helpless fetus: the mother's womb. It suggests that believers–and to a degree all of mankind–are nurtured in the safety of God's tender mercies by his loving kindness.

Grace, then, is an all-important element in the divine relationship with humanity and is the focus of blessing in the Scriptures. "Grace be unto you," was a common greeting,[1] as well as a frequent benediction,[2] from the apostles. This was in keeping with the Jewish tradition that a simple greeting took the form of a blessing. The fact that "*Shalom!*" is the common form of saying hello and good-bye among Jewish people may well be because the word *sha-*

lom is the concluding word of the Aaronic benediction.

Paul, in particular, asserted that the believer's very salvation was contingent upon God's grace: "For by grace have you been saved through faith."[3] The apostle also noted God's abundance of grace and his determination to provide grace even in the most dire of circumstances: "Where sin does abound, grace does much more abound."[4] When the knowledge of sin caused sin to be abundant, God's response was to expand the range of his grace to account for man's disobedience. He continued to draw men to himself, away from their sinful inclination and toward obedience to his instruction. He did so through his grace. This is why Paul was assured by the Lord: "My grace is sufficient for you."[5]

THE GRACE CONTINUUM

The principle of blessing and being blessed can be described as the "blessing continuum." The means by which the blessing is conveyed from God and is ultimately returned to him can be called the "grace continuum." This reciprocal nature of the blessing dynamic is best illustrated in a word study in the Apostolic Scriptures. The word for grace, which is the source and medium of the divine blessing, is χάρις (*charis*),[6] from which early Church Latin derived *charitas* (Anglicized as "charity"). Grace is the blessing that descends from God upon his people. It is the unmerited favor of God that is extended without condition to the one who is the object of God's love and blessing. God is always the source,[7] the fountainhead of both blessing and grace,[8] for it is not in the capacity of man to generate grace or blessing from within his own being.

Any lateral manifestation of blessing in men's lives is the direct result of the prior infusion of divine grace. Even the capacity to do good deeds apart from divine redemption and rebirth through the Messiah is a result of the implant of God's instructions in the hearts and minds of all men that itself is a gift of grace.[9] God's grace is given to all, and without it no life could be sustained. A far more abundant measure of grace is given to those who choose to believe in God's provision for their sins: they are saved by grace[10] and are given the full blessing of the Divine.

The grace does not, however, remain limited to the one whom God blesses. It is transferred laterally into the lives of others through the gifting of the Holy Spirit that God places in the lives of all he has added to his family of faith. The Greek word for the gifts that God gives as manifestations of the Spirit is χάρισμα (*charisma*, pl. *charismata*). These gifts are given for the benefit of the entire community of believers.[11] The *charismata* are given to individuals so that they can become channels of the divine grace.

The truth that grace is foundational to gifting as a means for the lateral transfer of God's blessing to the lives of others is confirmed in Paul's observation that believers have gifts that differ "according to the grace [*charis*] that is given to [them]."[12] The apostle continued to elaborate on the various *charismata* that were given through God's grace to the church. This is the same context in which he discussed the various manifestations of the Holy Spirit given for the profit of all believers.[13] In another discourse, Paul observed that "to every one of us grace is given according to the measure of the gift of Christ." The word for gift here is *dorea*, which speaks of the supernatural gifts that are given to believers, including the gift of eternal life.[14] The gift is imparted through the medium of God's grace. When that gift flows to others, it is still a manifestation of grace (*charis*) channeled by *charismata*.

God's blessing, then, is given so that the one who is divinely blessed may, in turn, be a blessing. The grace that is given vertically is to be channeled horizontally into the lives of others. In order to bless others, one must become a channel through which God's blessing can flow. Recognizing God as the ultimate source of all blessing will make the blesser humble about his own control over the capacity to bless. At the same time, however, it will empower him to become highly available as a channel of divine blessing.[15] The principle that was established in the life of Abraham becomes a paradigm for blessing as God wishes it to be applied in the lives of all his children. Abraham was blessed so that through him all nations could be blessed. All believers, likewise, are blessed in order to be the bearers of God's blessing.

The blessing that flows from one person to another by means of gifting in the Holy Spirit is also a reciprocal blessing. One cannot bless another without being blessed in return. The energy of the blessing is reflected from the blessed back to the blesser. In like manner, some blessings can have residual effects on many others over long periods of time. This can even produce generational blessing. The nature of blessing is such that it can never be bottled up. The benediction is so powerful that once unleashed it reverberates, taking the grace into totally unforeseen vistas through a chain reaction of blessing.

The blessing does not end in the transactional and reciprocal grace from the one who is blessed of God blessing others and, in turn, being blessed himself. What has flowed into the lives of men is returned to God who gave it. The grace continues to be manifest from simple divine impartation, through gifting, and finally returns to God in the form of thanksgiving. The Greek word for thanksgiving is εὐχαριστία (*eucharistia*), the word from which the term *eucharist* is derived. The believer who has received God's grace (*charis*) through the blessing of another's gift (*charisma*) is so blessed that he returns the blessing to God who gave it as thanksgiving (*eucharistia*). The blessing of grace is uncontainable! It must be released in reciprocity.

This was the dynamic that Paul succinctly described in this way: "In everything give thanks [*eucharistia*], for this is the will of God in Christ Jesus concerning you." It was not, however, a revolutionary, new idea that the apostle was expounding. It was but a continuation of the rich tradition of blessing God that this Jewish rabbi had been taught from infancy and later at the feet of Gamliel, the leading Jewish sage of his time.

Jewish tradition emphasizes the fact that it is essential for a believer to give thanks to God for every event and matter of life,[16] whether good or bad, so that perpetual thanksgiving flows from the mouth of the believer to God. The tradition is as ancient as Job who, when confronted with the greatest tragedy of his life, simply paused and blessed the Lord.[17] David shared the same passion for thanksgiving that Paul underscored: "I will bless the Lord at all times; his praise shall continually be in my mouth."[18] This connection between praise, thanksgiving, and blessing was emphasized to all observant Hebrews from antiquity. They were to bless God. As a matter of fact, the very formula of Jewish prayer is fundamentally a blessing, with each petition to God beginning with a blessing of his name, "Blessed are you, O Lord our God, King of the universe."

The thanksgiving that is offered to God is a means of capturing both the blessing and the grace that transmits that blessing and returning it to its source, the Almighty. "Blessings on the horizontal, earthly plane ultimately flow to and from the ultimate source of all blessing."[19] Blessing God throughout the day in every matter of life is a means of returning the blessing that has come down from heaven and completing the cycle of blessing and grace. It forms a continuum of blessing.

The blessing continuum, therefore, works by di-

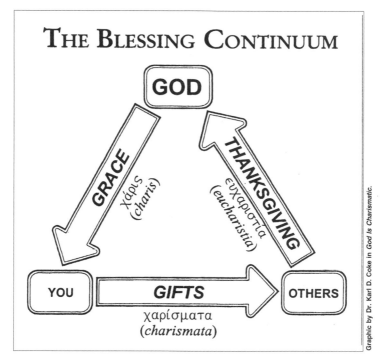

THE BLESSING CONTINUUM

GOD

GRACE
χάρις
(charis)

THANKSGIVING
εὐχαριστία
(eucharistia)

YOU — GIFTS — OTHERS
χαρίσματα
(charismata)

vine grace. *Charis* is given vertically to be manifest laterally through *charismata* and finally to be returned to God as *eucharistia*.

BLESSED TO BLESS

The blessing of God that is imparted to those who open themselves to his grace is, therefore, extended to others through the anointing and ministry that represents God's gift of grace in their lives. These humble souls have qualified themselves to be instruments through which the grace of God can flow into the lives of others. Like the patriarch of faith, Abraham, they are points of light and blessing. They do not consume the grace upon themselves but always release it both to men and to God. They are blessed of God with a view toward blessing others. God expects it, and so do they! They readily "work the works of

Abraham,"[20] doing justice and loving mercy and freely extending it to their fellow man. They do not omit the weightier matters of God's law, justice, mercy, and faith.[21] They treat others as they would prefer to be treated.[22] They love with the love that Christ loved,[23] that self-sacrificing love that transcends human reason. They imitate their God by becoming sources of blessing themselves. Like Abraham, they are commissioned to be God's blessing bearers.

[1] Romans 1:7; 1 Corinthians 1:3; Galatians 1:3; Ephesians 1:2; Philippians 1:2; Colossians 1:2; Titus 1:4; Philemon 1:3; 1 Peter 1:2; 2 Peter 1:2; 2 John 1:3.

[2] Romans 16:24; 1 Corinthians 16:23; Galatians 6:18; Ephesians 6:24; Philippians 4:23; Colossians 3:16; 1 Timothy 6:21; Titus 3:1; Hebrews 13:25.

[3] Ephesians 2:8.

[4] Romans 5:20.

[5] 2 Corinthians 12:9.

[6] The concept of the continuum of grace is from my friend, Karl D. Coke, and is featured in his excellent book, *God Is Charismatic* (Charlotte, NC: AndyBooks, 1983), p. 12.

[7] Colossians 1:18.

[8] Psalm 36:9.

[9] Romans 2:15.

[10] Ephesians 2:8.

[11] 1 Corinthians 12:7.

[12] Romans 12:6.

[13] 1 Corinthians 12:7.

[14] Romans 6:23.

[15] Daniel Alexander, "What is Blessing?" from the web site: *www.cbicville.org/sermons/rakn5762.html*, p. 5.

[16] Psalm 34:1.

[17] Job 1:21.

[18] Psalm 34:1.

[19] Ellen Davis, quoted in Alexander, "What is Blessing?", p. 8.

[20] John 8:39.

[21] Matthew 23:23.

[22] Matthew 7:12.

[23] John 13:34; 15:13.

Chapter 6

Blessing God

More often than not when Christians think of blessing, they imagine God's providing their emotional, spiritual, and material needs. They also think of blessing their food or having a priest bless things in order to make them holy. The focus of the Christian concept of blessing, then, is on man and things.

On the other hand, when Jews think of blessing, they do so in the context of the ancient and enduring Hebraic practice of blessing (praising) God.[1] Even when they enjoy material things and petition God for his favor upon themselves, their families, their communities, and the entire chosen people, they do so within the framework of the *berakhah*. This blessing framework is the *berakhot* system in which God is praised for every event of life, from the mundane to the sublime, including both the good and the bad that one experiences. The observant Jew has an outline of over one hundred specific expressions of praise that he can direct toward the Eternal throughout the day. The Mishnah's Tractate *Berakhot* lists such verbal reactions to scores of life's events.

Blessing is not merely a formula, the recitation of specific words. It is "the experience of entering through prayer and openness to God into a mode of existence where the paramount realities are God's goodness and God's power for making or doing good."[2] By focusing man's attention on the God who is good, the ongoing experience of blessing maintains a distinct God-consciousness in the soul and makes every moment of the day a sacred experience. Indeed, there is nothing that is not an opportunity for praising God.

BLESSING GOD AT ALL TIMES

It was the Psalmist of Israel who penned the immortal words of the hymn: "I will bless the Lord at all times: his praise shall continually be in my mouth."[3] The word *bless* is *barakh*, the root of the *berakhah* (blessing). It is parallel and synonymous with "praise" (*tehillah*), more specifically a song of praise. King David knew the value of constant praise to God in the form of blessing. The God-consciousness that continuous praise nurtures in the human heart is the foundation of the act of blessing or kneeling in reverence to the Almighty.

Perhaps David drew on the experience noted in the story of Job, an honorable man who endured one of the fiercest satanic onslaughts in history. Even in the face of his most tragic moment, Job declared: "The Lord has given, and the Lord has taken away; blessed be the name of the Lord."[4] Job's blessing was not a "gesture of submission to fate and inevitability but an act of rebellion against the seemingly victorious logic of destiny."[5] In a world where all too often God is praised only in times of success and prosperity, such a statement seems strange. Indeed, in some schemes of hyper-faith theology and prosperity gospel, it would seem ridiculous. Job recognized that he was entirely under the protection and provision of the Almighty. Though he had acquired wealth, he understood that God had given to him all that he had. If God had given, God could rightly take away. At any rate, whatever the situation or circumstance, God was to be praised; therefore, Job blessed the Lord.

The Mishnah insists that the blessings over good and bad news must be similar. For good news, a Jewish person says, "Blessed is the One who is good and bestows good." For bad tidings, particularly of a death, he says, "Blessed be the True Judge." God is praised for all things that occur in life because the believer knows that nothing is beyond God's purview.

This concept of continual praise toward God was reinforced in Paul's injunction to the Christian church: "Always be joyful; pray constantly; give thanks in all circumstances, for this is God's will for you in Christ Jesus."[6] Each of these instructions was based in Paul's rabbinic training from Gamliel. They are succinct statements of ancient Jewish worship through prayer and blessings.

Even though one may not always be happy, one can, nevertheless, be joyful, for joy is the satisfaction of knowing that God is in control and that all things work together for good to his elect. Prayer can be constant when one follows the biblical pattern that provides for hours of prayer morning, noon, and evening, the times that David set aside to pray[7] and the three times that Daniel prayed daily.[8] One can also give thanks in everything by practicing the Jewish order for blessing the Lord at all times, the *berakhot*.

BLESSING GOD FIRST

Before one enjoys anything of the human experience, before he blesses others, before he petitions for blessing, he must first bless God. The sages of Israel have suggested that to enjoy anything without first blessing God is akin to blasphemy. A God-conscious people will always think of God first before they consider themselves or their surroundings. A God-centered life is destined to be a life of blessing, as Abraham of old came to understand. The old maxim has never been more true: "God first, others second, self last."

The worship of God from a Hebraic perspective begins with blessing God. The *berakhot* are the "generative nucleus"[9] of the three elements of Jewish worship's delivery system: the *Shema*, the *Tefillah* (prayer), and the *Keri'at Torah* (reading of Torah). All of these exercises begin with the blessing of God and are focused on God, not man. They set the tone in the Jewish heart for awe and reverence toward the

Almighty. The Jewish mindset directs attention to God first.

Because the *Shema* summarizes monotheism as the cornerstone of all biblical faith, it is the most prominent declaration in Jewish worship, declaring "Hear, O Israel, the Lord our God, the Lord is one. Love the Lord your God with all your heart and with all your soul and with all your strength."[10] It encapsulates the revelation that Abraham received that which was foundational to his divine call and the subsequent covenant and blessing.

That Jesus should recognize the *Shema* as the prime commandment should have come as no surprise, for he was immersed in Judaism's rich tradition of ethical monotheism by teaching in home, synagogue, and temple. When queried about the greatest of the commandments, Jesus immediately recited the *Shema*[11] and declared twice that it was the first in rank. One can never proceed to additional knowledge about God or true worship of God unless he has passed the Abrahamic test and knows that God is one.

The central prayer in Jewish life is called simply *ha-Tefillah* (the Prayer). Interestingly enough, it is composed of eighteen benedictions, not mere petitions! The consensus of scholarship is that this prayer originated in the second century before the time of Jesus. It is said that these eighteen blessings of the *Tefillah* were composed by 120 elders, many of whom were prophets. It is certain that Jesus and the apostles prayed some form of this prayer of blessings in their faithful attendance in Israel's synagogues. This prayer of blessings has remained so important to the Jewish people that it is always prayed with each worshiper standing facing Jerusalem (hence, its alternate name *Amidah*, meaning "standing"). The act of praying while standing is an indication of the worshipers' readiness to receive and obey God's instructions.

The word *tefillah* (the prayer of blessings) is rooted in the word *palal*, which means to "judge, study, or test" (literally, "to roll out flat"). It implies "judging oneself," a concept echoed in Paul's observation: "If we judged ourselves rightly, we should not be judged"[12] and his injunction that every man should "judge himself."[13] The apostle's rabbinic training had acquainted him with the true nature of Jewish prayer as a confrontation with the Divine and his Word wherein the "soul discovers its identity and frees itself from the incrustations and mystifications that keep it alienated" from God.[14] Prayer in this early Judaeo-Christian tradition was not a sentimental journey of pious platitudes and pitiful petitions. It was a fine tuning of the conscience through application of the living Word of God (Torah), the process that is also called sanctification and walking with God. The entire function of prayer in Jewish tradition is encapsulated in the first petition of the "Lord's Prayer," which states, "Thy will be done."

In each of the blessings, God is blessed first for one or more of his qualities or the elements of his character and his provision for his people. The first three define God's innermost being: loving kindness (*chesed*), power (*gevurah*), and holiness (*kedushah*). The final three benedictions express the themes of gratitude, the hope of restoration, and abundant peace. The twelve intermediate blessings deal with understanding, repentance, forgiveness, freedom, bodily health, abundance of the earth, reunification of the scattered, justice, punishment of enemies,[15] reward for the just, the new Jerusalem, the Messiah, and hearing of prayers.

Interestingly enough, only the first three and the last three blessings, along with a blessing of thanks for holy days, are offered on the Sabbath and on festival days. The intermediate petitionary blessings are omitted because God alone is the focus on the days of appointment when he has promised to meet with his children. This takes the theme of focus on blessing God and not on men's needs to a higher plane. It puts God first and extols and exalts his holy name.

TRACTATE *BERAKHOT*

It should come as no surprise that the very first section of the Mishnah, the foundation of that great corpus of Jewish biblical and traditional commentary called the Talmud,[16] is Tractate *Berakhot*. The first three of its nine chapters focus on the *Shema*. The fourth and fifth discuss prayer in general while the next three deal with the *Birkat haMazon*, the blessing of God after the meal. The final chapter deals with other benedictions. The first tractate in the Talmud, then, focuses on the blessings of God that are central to Jewish life and worship.

The *berakhot* are the beginning of the Mishnah, not simply because the subject is the first part of Jewish thought, but because the *berakhot* are its foundation, the matrix from which the rest of the Talmud emerges. The *berakhot* are the "foundation stone" of Jewish liturgy.[17] This fact contains an invaluable lesson for Christians whose faith emerged from the matrix of the Second Temple Judaism. Blessings of God are fundamental to all authentic religious experience.

THE *BERAKHAH*

The traditional blessing in Judaism begins with the phrase, "Blessed are you, O Lord our God, King of the universe, who has sanctified us by his commandments . . ." This formula for blessing God both addresses God directly and speaks of him in the third person. The sages have spoken to this inconsistency of language by suggesting that the blessing formula recognizes both the immanence and the transcendence of God. The one God of the Bible is first understood in terms of his relationship with his people. The King of the universe is "our God." It is possible for believers in him to have a personal and dialogical relationship with God with the understanding of his loving, paternal nearness to his children. On the other hand, however, God is utterly holy, wholly other, inscrutable, and beyond man's comprehension, he who has sanctified us by his commandments.

In its opening words, then, the *berakhah* reveals profound understanding of God's relationship with man, one that is both immanent and transcendent. "A God who was only 'present' would become an 'idol' for human beings;

instead of serving him they would make use of him. A god who was only absent would become alien to human beings: instead of calling upon him they would ignore him."[18] When the Jewish people bless God as both personal ("you") and impersonal ("his"), they worship the God who is both Father to his family and King of the universe.

BLESS GOD!

Being a just, Torah-observant Jew, James noted that Christians "bless God."[19] David commanded the people to "bless God in the congregations."[20] He encouraged them to "sing unto the Lord and bless his name."[21] Even the entrance into the gates of God's sanctuary should be accompanied by blessings to the name of God.[22] David encouraged a graphic and physical demonstration of blessing: "Lift up your hands in the sanctuary, and bless the Lord."[23] The blessing of God in Judaeo-Christian tradition was not to be a casual mental exercise. "Bless the Lord, O my soul: and all that is within me, bless his holy name!" the Psalmist exclaimed.[24] These words were an oft-repeated theme[25] of self-exhortation to praise, for David continued to urge the holy angels and the hosts of ministers to bless God as well, and he concluded his hymn by saying that all God's works everywhere in his dominion should bless his holy name.[26]

The blessing of God is not an occasional exercise of pompous piety. "Every day I will bless you, and praise your name for ever and ever,"[27] David declared. Blessing "is not a feeling but objective thinking based on divine viewpoint."[28] Anyone who is in his right mind will bless God as evidenced by the fact that Nebuchadnezzar "blessed the Most High" when, after seven years of insanity, he was restored to a sound mind.[29]

Blessing God is an exercise of the whole person, both a mental and a visceral action that is exercised every day, and even then, it is not just a once-a-day exercise. "Seven times a day I praise you for your upright judgments,"[30] David declared. When Christians come to recognize the rich Hebraic blessing heritage that was foundational to the faith of Jesus and the apostles, they too will "bless the Lord at all times" and will find themselves "giving thanks" in all things.[31]

[1] God himself is the source of all blessing. Mankind can bless God only in the sense of praising or glorifying him. Humanity can never be a source of blessing *for* God.

[2] Ellen Davis, quoted in Alexander, "What is Blessing?"

[3] Psalm 34:1.

[4] Job 1:21, TNK.

[5] Carmine di Sante, *Jewish Prayer: The Origins of the Christian Liturgy* (Mahwah, NJ: Paulist Press, 1985), p. 40.

[6] 1 Thessalonians 5:16-17, NJB; 5:18a, NRS; 5:18b, NASB.

[7] Psalm 55:17.

[8] Daniel 6:10.

[9] di Sante, p. 33.

[10] Deuteronomy 6:4-5, NIV.

[11] Mark 12:29-30.

[12] 1 Corinthians 11:31, NASB.

[13] 1 Corinthians 11:28.

[14] di Sante, p. 79.

[15] This benediction is actually a malediction that was added to the "Eighteen" (perhaps in the first century) as a means of bringing judgment upon heretics.

[16] The term *Talmud* is an abbreviation of *Talmud Torah*, meaning "study of divine instruction (law)."

[17] A. E. Millgram, *Jewish Prayer* (Philadelphia: Jewish Publication Society of America, 1971), p. 92.

[18] di Sante, p. 49.

[19] James 3:9.

[20] Psalm 68:26.

[21] Psalm 96:2.

[22] Psalm 100:4.

[23] Psalm 134:2.

[24] Psalm 103:1.

[25] Psalm 104:35.

[26] Psalm 103:22.

[27] Psalm 145:2.

[28] Elmer Towns, "Applying the Blessing," from the web site: *www.realtime.net/~wdoud/topics/blessing.html*, p. 4.

[29] Daniel 4:33-34.

[30] Psalm 119:164, NJB.

[31] 1 Thessalonians 5:16, 18.

Chapter 7

Blessing Others

While biblical blessing is first directed vertically from God to man and from man to God (like the proverbial ladder from heaven to earth), it is also manifest laterally from one human to another. This practice was seen in Abraham's life when he was blessed by Melchizedek.[1] It was repeated in the lives of the patriarchs when they were blessed by their fathers. It was a continuing practice of prophets, priests, and kings. Moses pronounced a benediction upon the twelve tribes of Israel.[2] Because man is made in the image of the Creator, he is inherently predisposed to bless others. In ancient times, therefore, people regularly blessed one another and their homes, their labors, their land, and their possessions.

The idea of placing the blessing of God upon others, saying, "The blessing of the Lord be upon you; we bless you in the name of the Lord,"[3] is referenced by David as one of the chief advantages that those who are in opposition to God's Word and will do not possess. Such a statement must have been common among the Israelites at that time. This goes beyond the blessing of Israelites by the sons of Aaron and the blessing of children by parents. It was an ongoing tradition of adding God's blessing to others as a means of greeting, during the course of dialogue, and as a form of good-bye.[4] A good example of blessing as greeting is seen in the statement that Saul went out to welcome Samuel, which literally says, "[He] went to meet him and to bless him."[5] When Boaz blessed his workers, saying "The Lord be with you," they replied, "The Lord bless you."[6]

THE POWER OF WORDS

Words are creative, as well as destructive. They can build up, and they can tear down. Just as God's Word is a living, active, creative power, so men's words generate either good or evil. Solomon noted this truth: "Through the blessing of the upright a city is exalted, but by the mouth of the wicked it is destroyed."[7] Those who are righteous in God's sight not only have the right, but also the responsibility to speak those blessings into the community. The benediction brings life and prosperity to those who are its object because it speaks God's Word into their lives. Solomon noted the impact of God's blessing: "The blessing of the Lord brings wealth."[8]

If spoken words can exalt or destroy a city, they certainly can also impact the lives of individuals. This is why it is important that believers exercise care to speak blessings and not curses. Because of his understanding of the power of words, Paul gave this injunction: "Let no unwholesome word proceed from your mouth, but only such a word as is good for edification according to the need of the moment, that it may give grace to those who hear."[9] Benediction (blessing) is the good word that transmits grace to those who hear it.

Both Jesus and Paul even exhorted believers to bless those who curse them: "Bless those who curse you, pray for those who mistreat you."[10] James warned Christians against blessing God while cursing men and wondered how both blessings and curses can come from the same mouth.[11] David shamed those who bless with the mouth while cursing with the heart.[12] Right relationship with God will eventuate in right relationship with man and place God's blessings on others with a pure heart of blessing.

RISKING A BLESSING

More often than not, Christians are reluctant to speak blessing into the lives of others, especially God's blessing. While they may wish others well in a purely social sense, they do not understand that their status before God empowers them to bless others in God's name. What if the Christian church around the world were to say to all its members and to all humankind everywhere: "The blessing of the Lord be upon you: we bless you in the name of the Lord"? What a profound impact such a universally spoken benediction would have both on believers and on those who do not profess faith in Jesus!

Believers who have insight into God's plan for interpersonal blessings may still be challenged by self doubts and fear of failure. This is where one has to stand on the authority of God's Word and risk bestowing a blessing on another person. Blessing, therefore, is an act of faith. It is the act of taking the risk of believing God and sharing anointing with others. Blessing God is easy. God's bounty is so manifest in individual lives that praise toward him is a natural reaction. What believers need to know in blessing God is only form and substance. Blessing others, however, is a challenge that requires commitment laterally to people who are a tangible, present reality. It demands both faith in God and faith in others.

BESTOWING A BLESSING

If blessing is to be transmitted, someone must do it. Good wishes and good thoughts are insufficient. Someone must act. That someone is every believer. Accept the challenge. Bestow a blessing. Reach out and touch someone. Lay hands on their head, grasp their hand, clutch their shoulder. Respectful human touch means one is seeking to con-

nect, not to keep one's distance. Step up, look into their
eyes, and speak words that the mind and the Holy Spirit
frame. Written blessings can produce results; however, spoken blessings are more powerful. It does not matter whether
the statement is fluent or eloquent. It may be halting and
even jumbled. What is important is that it is spoken, that
the one who is blessed feels the words vibrating in his ear, in
his mind, and in his soul. Affirm what you discern to be godly
qualities in that person and speak what you envision through
the Holy Spirit as God's blessing in that life. Give the reassurance that God will bring to pass his blessing as he has promised and that you will be a part of God's continuing blessing
for that person.

When you begin to bless others, you share in the
Abrahamic blessing by being a channel of blessing. You
also share in the rich biblically Hebraic heritage of Jesus
and the apostles.

A Blessing Formula

Looking the person in the eye and making a meaning-
ful touch by grasping his hand, or laying your hand on her
head, say:

*"The blessing of the Lord be upon you: I bless you in
the name of the Lord. May you be like Ephraim and
Manasseh (for males). May you be like Sarah and Rebecca,
like Rachel and Leah (for females). The Lord bless you
and keep you. The Lord cause his face to shine upon you
and be gracious unto you. The Lord turn his face toward
you and give you peace. May the Spirit of the Lord, the
spirit of wisdom, the spirit of understanding, the spirit of
counsel, the spirit of power, the spirit of knowledge, and
the spirit of the fear of the Lord rest upon you."*

You may conclude by "giving the blessing appropriate"[13]
to the person as you are inspired by the Holy Spirit.

[1] Genesis 14:19.
[2] Deuteronomy 33:1ff.

[3] Psalm 129:8.

[4] Nehemiah Pollen, quoted in Alexander, "What is Blessing?", p. 2.

[5] 1 Samuel 13:10. Virtually every version of the Bible translates this as "meet and welcome." Literally it is *"likrato l'barakho,"* "meet and bless."

[6] Ruth 2:4.

[7] Proverbs 11:11, NIV.

[8] Proverbs 10:22, NIV.

[9] Ephesians 4:29, NASB.

[10] Luke 6:28, NIV; Romans 12:14.

[11] James 3:9-10.

[12] Psalm 62:4.

[13] Genesis 49:28.

Chapter 8

The Posture of Blessing

If one is to receive blessing from God or extend blessing to others, a certain attitude must be developed and maintained. This posture of blessing is clearly revealed in the fact that the Hebrew word for blessing, בְּרָכָה (*berakhah*), comes from the verbal root, בֶּרֶךְ (*berek*), which means "knee."[1] The word בַּרַךְ (*barak*) means "to kneel." The concept is that of kneeling before a superior, particularly God. In ancient times, petitioners would kneel before the king to demonstrate their fealty and submission and to seek favor.

There is profound poetic imagery in the use of the word *berakhah* to describe God's relationship with man that brings grace and benediction into human lives. *Berakhah* paints a wonderful portrait of God in his infinite tender mercy kneeling in order to reach down to his weak, suffering children and to lavish his loving kindness upon them. God is king, but he is also father, and as father, he is intent upon reaching down to his children and showering them with his infinite blessings.

God himself, then, has set the example of blessing's posture by reaching down to humanity and lifting them up. One can neither receive a blessing nor be a blessing without first being humble and submitted either to the one who is bestowing a blessing or to the one being blessed.

The bent knee is the root of the blessing. Humility and submission are the beginning point for blessing God and man.

THE ATTITUDE OF GRACE AND BLESSING

The action of gratitude manifest in continually blessing God and returning the grace that he has given to its source is fundamental to the attitude of blessing. Both James and Peter, two of the earliest church's most prominent leaders, affirmed that "God gives grace to the humble," while he "resists the proud."[2] The word for *humble* in Greek is ταπεινός (*tapeinos*), which means "not rising from the ground." It is symbolic of the attitude of complete submission to God's will. In biblical times, the word *worship* also indicated prostration in the divine presence. Both the Hebrew שָׁחָה (*shachah*) and the Greek προσκυνέω (*proskuneo*) mean "to prostrate oneself," with the Greek even offering the metaphor of a dog licking its master's hand. Humility, then, is essential to worship.

The word בָּרַךְ (*barak*) especially confirms that the posture of blessing is manifest in genuflection, kneeling in humility, worship, and adoration to the Divine. When one blesses (*barak*) God through worship (*shachah*), he is the recipient of God's grace (*chesed, charis*). When one is arrogant and self-sufficient, he is rejected and resisted by a God of grace. Solomon noted that "a man's pride shall bring him low: but honor shall uphold the humble in spirit."[3] Jesus observed that "whosoever shall humble himself as a little child, the same shall be great in the kingdom of heaven."[4] James, therefore, exhorted the believers, "Humble yourselves in the sight of the Lord, and he shall lift you up."[5] God shields the humble with his grace and lifts up their heads.[6]

The bent knee physically manifests the posture of submission, one of the most important qualities that a believer can manifest. Submission to God is foundational to receiving every spiritual blessing. It is an acknowledgment that one is subservient to God's will. It was apropos, then, for James to exhort, "Submit yourselves, then, to God. . . . Come near to God and he will come near to you."[7] The apostle made this declaration in the same breath in which he declared that God gives grace to the humble. When believers approach God with submission and humility, he comes near to them to impart his grace and benediction.

Blessing God is an act of genuflection. One may not physically kneel, but he is truly humbled in his heart. Blessing in Jewish tradition is a manifestation that one sees God's utter holiness, his complete otherness. It is an acknowledgment that God is the creator and is, therefore, outside creation, and that God is eternal, infinitely beyond the temporal.

Submission does not end with the knee bowed to God. Believers are exhorted then to "submit to one another out of reverence for Christ."[8] Paul immediately prefaced this instruction with these words: "Always [give] thanks to God the Father for everything, in the name of our Lord Jesus Christ."[9] One blesses God first and immediately submits to others out of reverence for Christ.

THE SERVANT MINDSET

When believers are subject to one another, blessing one another with God's benediction is truly efficacious. The one who is bestowing the blessing and the one who is receiving it must be submitted mutually in order for God's blessing and gift to flow laterally between them. The one who is being blessed must recognize his fellow believer as God's servant who has received God's grace for him. The one who is blessing must submit himself to his fellow believer, understanding that what he imparts is only what he

The Hebrew letter *gimel* is a pictograph of a camel, a symbol of blessing in the ancient world. In order for the camel to unload a blessing or be loaded with a blessing, it must kneel. The kneeling camel is a memorable graphic demonstration of the posture of blessing.

Graphic concept from Dr. Karl D. Coke

has received from God's grace and that as God's servant, he is also the servant of his fellow believer.

It should be noted that the title of choice among the apostles was uniformly "slave," often translated "servant," but clearly "slave" from the Greek δουλος (*doulos*). The word δουλος translates the Hebrew word עֶבֶד (*eved*) which was used to describe the Israelites' slavery to Pharaoh. When individuals come to faith in Jesus as Messiah, they become love slaves according to the ancient formula.[10] Believers are not their own; therefore, they have no occasion for self-exaltation. The greatest among them is the slave of all.[11]

THINKING SOBERLY

God does not, however, require his children to grovel before him, debasing themselves and destroying their sense of personhood. He created man with a sense of dignity and self-worth. It is only when that natural status is inflated through the sin of pride that it becomes an enemy of God akin to the primal adversary who was first lifted up in an escalating pride that eventually sought equality with God himself.[12] The arrogance that caused Lucifer to be expelled from God's presence will also cast those who replicate it away from God and his blessing.

The Jewish people have understood the importance of humility in their approach to God and of servanthood in their approach to others; however, they have not been swept into the level of self-deprecation that destroys one's sense of self-worth. Christians, on the other hand, have often stretched unworthiness to the point of worthlessness. This has led to extreme acts of self-abnegation and self-flagellation that are emotionally and physically unhealthy and are spiritually bankrupt.

How is one to maintain the balance of humility that God seeks without lowering oneself into an abysmal state of hopelessness? How low is too low? The answer is found in Paul's very Jewish response to this issue: "Never pride yourself on being better than you really are, but think of yourself dispassionately, recognizing that God has given to each one his measure of faith."[13] The exhortation is first to humility; however, it secondly urges balance so that one does not think of himself more lowly than he should. The Greek word Paul uses is σοφρονέω (*sophroneo*), which means to be of a sound mind or to make a moderate estimate of oneself. It implies making a fair accounting of one's capabilities, weighing assets and liabilities.

How does one make such an accounting? The answer is in the previous verse: "Be transformed by the renewing of your mind, that you may prove what the will of God is."[14] A sober, well-balanced evaluation is what is needed when approaching God. It can be achieved only when one recognizes that the gift of God's grace is operative in his life. Such an evaluation empowers one to approach God in humility while at the same time coming boldly before the throne of grace,[15] where grace for every need and blessing upon blessing will be found.

VULNERABILITY, THE PLANE OF BLESSING

Submission always places one in a posture of vulnerability. Humans do not relish vulnerability and will instinctively do everything possible to limit their exposure to the possibility of exploitation. In Christ, however, one must understand that vulnerability is the only position from which ministry and blessing can flow. When one is humbly submitted on bent knee, he cannot flee from danger, nor can he readily fight against it.

Even God himself could not fully manifest his blessing for man until he became vulnerable in the person of his only begotten Son. When God was manifest in the flesh[16] in the incarnation of Jesus, for the first time he became vulnerable to the temptation of sin,[17] to suffering,[18] and ultimately to death.[19] In subjecting himself to human flesh, Jesus humbled himself and forever demonstrated the "mind of Christ."[20] Though he inherently shared coequality with the Father, he did not grasp at his status but humbled himself and died on the cross so that he might redeem humanity from the bondage of sin and death. Jesus had to die in order to bring the blessing of eternal life to all who believe.

Abraham and Sarah became vulnerable when they left family and land and crossed over into a strange place. Abraham searched for a city of which God was the architect,[21] and he never found it while on earth. He was promised land, yet he personally had none except a family cemetery that he purchased. He was a pilgrim and a stranger and was called an alien. He knew the pain of vulnerability. Because he ventured into the unknown in response to the divine command, God said to Abraham, "I will make your name great."[22] When he humbled himself and endured the pain of vulnerability, God gave to Abraham the very thing for which the proto-Babylonians had been judged when they tried to build their ziggurat to heaven, saying, "Let us make a name for ourselves."[23]

It has been rightly said, therefore, that one must bleed before he can bless. It is only when one is willing to pour his life out in service to others that he has the potential to bring God's blessing and grace into their lives. One must submit to God's will and to the needs of others in order to be an instrument of God's grace and blessing. In like manner, the one who has need must submit to God and to other believers, denying self-sufficiency and acknowledging dependence upon God and others. Self-sufficiency fuels a spirit of pride which both God and others resist. Humility and submission draw both God and others to the side of the one who has need.

It is no wonder, then, that the posture of blessing is the bent knee. Genuflection places one in the posture to be blessed of God and to be an instrument of God's blessing to others. It also breaks down the spirit of pride and in its place nurtures the humility to which God and man are drawn to impart blessing and grace.

[1] Camels are said to *"barak"* (kneel) in Genesis 24:11.

[2] James 4:6; 1 Peter 5:5.
[3] Proverbs 29:23, KJV.
[4] Matthew 18:4.
[5] James 4:10.
[6] Psalm 3:3.
[7] James 4:7, KJV; 4:8, NIV.
[8] Ephesians 5:21, NIV.
[9] Ephesians 5:20, NIV.
[10] Exodus 21:6.
[11] Matthew 23:11.
[12] Isaiah 14:12-14; Ezekiel 28:14-15.
[13] Romans 12:3, NJB (New Jerusalem Bible).
[14] Romans 12:2, NASB.
[15] Hebrews 4:16.
[16] 1 Timothy 3:16.
[17] Hebrews 4:15.
[18] Hebrews 5:8.
[19] Hebrews 2:9.
[20] Philippians 2:5-8.
[21] Hebrews 11:10.
[22] Genesis 12:2.
[23] Genesis 11:4.

Chapter 9
A Shield of Blessing

God's blessing as a shield against the forces of evil was manifest in the ancient shield of David, the *Magen David*. While the modern *Magen David* is the six-pointed star that has come to symbolize the Jewish community and the state of Israel, the ancient shield of King David was likely an entirely different symbol. The Psalmist's military armor contained a design that is a paradigm of protection in the midst of even the most serious adversity.

David's shield was said to have been made of gold with a raised menorah engraved thereon. The menorah was the seven-branched lampstand that was designed by God himself[1] and was the sole means of illumination in Israel's sanctuaries. It was God's gift to Israel as a graphic demonstration that the light of the divine presence was continually focused on the chosen people. It was also a symbol that God had chosen to illustrate the fact that Israel was to be a light to the nations of the world. As the *ner tamid* (eternal light), it even came to represent the Eternal himself who is ever present with his people. It also established the fact that Israel's power was not in military devices but in the manifestation of the Eternal Light in their midst.

Generations after David's reign, the prophet Zechariah was given a graphic vision of a golden menorah with the accompanying divine message: "Not by might, nor by power, but by my Spirit, says the Lord."[2] It has been suggested that this message appeared in tongues of fire atop the menorah, for the message in Hebrew is precisely seven words, one for each of the menorah's lamps. Both the vision and the message confirm the fact that Israel's mission in the earth is not ensured by military might or political power. It is rather based in the manifestation of the divine light. God's light always conquers Satan's might.

It is also believed that in addition to the golden menorah emblazoned on David's shield, these words were also inscribed thereon: "God be merciful unto us, and bless us; and cause his face to shine upon us."[3] These lyrics that the king recorded in a song were merely a paraphrase of the divine priestly blessing in the form of a prayer. The opening refrain of that hymn was recapitulated in the psalm's concluding verse: "God, even our own God, shall bless us. God shall bless us; and all the ends of the earth shall fear him."[4]

David and his subjects were so convinced of the power of God's blessing that they even inscribed that blessing in petitionary form on the very shields of

Graphic by Peter Sherburne

The *Magen David*, the shield that King David used, was different from the six-pointed Star of David today. It likely was inscribed with a golden menorah and the words of the Divine Blessing. David's shield illustrates graphically that God's blessing is a shield to whose who bear it in their lives.

their military armor. Their faith in God's protection rested on the foundation of their covenant with God and on the divine blessing that continually accompanied that covenant. What better means of confirming their faith than to place that blessing foremost in the face of the enemy's onslaught! It was a way of saying, "God's light shields us from your might."

GOD HIMSELF, THE SHIELD

The idea of the blessing as a shield against every curse was confirmed in Abraham who was assured by God, "I am your shield."[5] The Lord himself is called the *magen* (shield) of Israel.[6] David said with confidence, "You, O Lord, are a shield about me,"[7] and he sang of God's blessing: "Surely you bless the righteous man, O Lord, encompassing him with favor like a shield."[8] King David understood that the blessing was a shield of divine favor. He also understood that God's truth was a shield.[9] God himself, the personification of truth, surrounds his favored people, enshrouding them in his blessing and thereby shielding them from attack.

The shield of faith[10] is based on the promises of God's Word and is activated when the believer blesses those who are covenanted with him. Faith, indeed, proceeds from hearing God's Word.[11] It is the Word that generates faith in the hearts of believers, and it is faith that emboldens them to access the divine presence and receive God's blessing, with its attendant spiritual and material benefits.

THE BLESSING SHIELDS FROM CURSES

The forces of evil constantly target humanity with maledictions. The enemy of men's souls seeks vulnerable sites to wreak havoc, to kill, steal, and destroy.[12] He assails his victims with the powers of deception, enticing and tempting them to rebel against divine instruction. He curses all mankind, but he reserves his most powerful salvos for the righteous. If he discovers even a small chink in their armor, he immediately attacks, hurling missiles of imprecation at the points of vulnerability.

The believer who remains in faithful partnership with God's covenant is shielded from those attacks by the divine blessing that proceeds from that covenant. First, he is not ignorant of Satan's devices,[13] for he has immersed himself in the God-breathed Scriptures that have equipped him for every good work.[14] Satan can gain no advantage over him[15] in the conflict of mind, soul, and body, for he has hidden God's Word in his heart so that he might not sin against his Lord.[16] Faith in God's promise is his shield of protection from the enemy's violent assault.[17]

The individualization of this divine truth for each believer is graphically demonstrated in God's ongoing protection of the Israelites from the maledictions of their enemies. Blessing rests upon the corporate body of Israel because of God's covenant, promise, and blessing to Abraham. His descendants were blessed with the same blessing that the patriarch received. In like manner, God cursed both Satan and those who cursed Israel.

The fledgling nation was journeying from Sinai where they had received the Torah as their national constitution. They were close to the Promised Land, the real estate inheritance that had been conveyed to Abraham in consideration of his faith. As they marched toward that land, their reputation preceded them. Balak, the king of Moab, was fearful of their impact upon his fiefdom because his land was in their path. Within the context of his religious experience, he believed that he could halt their forward march by assailing them with curses.

In order to implement this strategy, Balak sought to engage the services of the prophet Balaam as a cursing consultant. When this prophet-for-hire inquired of God about accepting the assignment, he was specifically forbidden from doing so and refused even to give the king an audience.

Upon Balak's insistence, however, Balaam visited the king and was offered a significant fee in exchange for his cursing exercise. His immediate response to the offer was, "If Balak would give me his house full of silver and gold, I cannot go beyond the word of the Lord my God, to do less or more."[18]

Tempted by the promised reward, however, Balaam, along with Balak, sought a high place from which he could launch maledictions against Israel. A series of promising locations were explored; however, the result was always the same. The king even requested that if the prophet could not curse Israel, at least he should not bless Israel.[19] At last, in desperation, Balaam repeated his original observation, "Even if Balak gave me his palace filled with silver and gold, I could not do anything of my own accord, good or bad, to go beyond the command of the Lord–and I must say only what the Lord says."[20]

It seemed that every time the hired gun summoned all of his strength to launch missiles of malediction, he discovered when he opened his mouth, regardless of his location, the only thing that would come forth from his lips was blessing. He even uttered the immortal messianic proclamation: "What I see for them is not yet, what I behold will not be soon: A star rises from Jacob, a scepter comes forth from Israel; it smashes the brow of Moab, the foundation of all children of Seth."[21] Thus the ultimate blessing upon Israel was declared by an avaricious prophet in the employ of Israel's enemy. The Star of Jacob is King Messiah, whose scepter is an instrument of righteousness[22] that will judge the entire earth and destroy all those who curse Israel by returning their curses against them sevenfold. As he promised Abraham, God will curse those who curse his people.

Ultimately, Balaam discovered the tragedy that awaits those who even attempt to curse those who are blessed of God. He was killed in battle, as the proposed curses returned to the one who dared to devise them. Not only did the discredited prophet die; those who sympathized with his ideas, including some among the camp of Israel, also paid the ultimate price. When God has blessed his people, the enemy cannot even successfully engage an apostate prophet to curse them. The blessing is so powerful and so encases God's covenant people that the enemy cannot penetrate the canopy of the blessing with the missiles of his curses. The imprecations that he devises issue forth as blessings instead.

THE CURSE REVERSE

When Nehemiah recounted the story of Balaam's attempt to curse Israel, he made this unusual observation: "Our God turned the curse into a blessing,"[23] reiterating what God himself had said to Israel.[24] Surely only God has the power to intercept a malediction and turn it into a benediction! As with the case of Joseph's brothers, what they had meant for evil, God intended for good.[25] God ensures that whatever happens in the life of the believer works together toward his benefit.[26]

God himself reverses the curse. When mankind was enslaved under the bondage of sin and death and was subject to the curses that God's law pronounced upon those who sinned by transgressing that law, God sent his Son to reverse the curse. Jesus accomplished this task by becoming a curse himself[27] and by assuming to himself all the curses for humanity's iniquities as he hung on the cross.[28] Jesus literally became sin[29] as the sins of all humanity of all ages were laid on him. By absorbing all the sin and all the curses, he was able to provide the efficacious atonement that returns those who believe to right relationship with the Father where they can receive his everlasting blessing.

What remains for the believer is God's blessing. These include those wonderful promises that Jesus made in the Sermon on the Mount called the "Beatitudes." The blessing that is imparted when the righteousness of Jesus is imputed to the believer for his faith is an irrevocable blessing. Jesus, the curse reverse, is the shield of the believer and is forever with each believer, even to the end of the age.[30] This is a shield of blessing that transcends mortal life and promises unparalleled blessing in the resurrection.

In the world to come, the believer will experience the blessing of the river of the water of life that flows from God's throne and will be given right to partake of the tree of life that was offered to Adam and Eve in the beginning. In this setting of the restored Garden of Eden, there will be no more curse, for they will have God's name written in their foreheads and will forever bask in the glory of his countenance. In this state of bliss, they will reign for ever and ever.[31]

SHIELDS UP!

What was true for ancient Israel in the wilderness is true for all who bear allegiance to the God of Israel. When they are walking in covenant submission to the Eternal, they are insulated from the enemy's curses. Only when they allow sins of disobedience and rebellion to create a breach in their divine covering is a channel opened for the curse to impact their lives. Even in man's weakness, though, God's strength is manifest. As Jesus comforted Paul, so he encourages the believer: "My grace is sufficient for you, for my strength is made perfect in weakness."[32]

The shield of faith is so effective that no weapon can ever succeed against it.[33] If God was Abraham's shield 4,000 years ago,[34] he is still the believer's defense today.[35] When the enemy advances like a flood, the Lord lifts up a battle standard against him,[36] an ensign of the heavenly, invulnerable kingdom. Even as he passes into the unknown territory of death and the life to come, the believer is secure, for God is with him.[37] Like the blessing on David's shield, the divine benediction that covers the believer preserves him from every attack, both in life and in death. God's shield protects!

[1] Exodus 25:31-37.
[2] Zechariah 4:6.
[3] Psalm 67:1, KJV.
[4] Psalm 67:6-7, KJV.
[5] Genesis 15:1.
[6] Deuteronomy 33:29.
[7] Psalm 3:3, JPS *Tanakh*.
[8] Psalm 5:12.
[9] Psalm 91:4.
[10] Ephesians 6:16.
[11] Romans 10:17.
[12] John 10:10.
[13] 2 Corinthians 2:11.
[14] 2 Timothy 3:16-17.
[15] 2 Corinthians 2:11.
[16] Psalm 119:11.
[17] Ephesians 6:16.
[18] Numbers 22:18, KJV.
[19] Numbers 23:25.
[20] Numbers 24:13, NIV
[21] Numbers 24:17, JPS *Tanakh*.
[22] Psalm 45:6; Hebrews 1:8.
[23] Nehemiah 13:2.
[24] Deuteronomy 23:5.
[25] Genesis 50:20.
[26] Romans 8:28.
[27] Galatians 3:13.
[28] Isaiah 53:5-6.
[29] 2 Corinthians 5:21.
[30] Matthew 28:20.
[31] Revelation 22:1-7.
[32] 2 Corinthians 12:9.
[33] Isaiah 54:17.
[34] Genesis 15:1.
[35] Psalm 94:22.
[36] Isaiah 59:19.
[37] Psalm 23:4.

Chapter 10

Blessing
Bandits

While it is always God's intention to bless his children, the forces of evil constantly position themselves to steal the blessing that God has promised and is in the process of bestowing. More often than not, God's promises are fulfilled over a period of time; therefore, patient endurance[1] or relying upon the promise is necessary for its full realization. Satan and his forces are well aware of this fact and seek to disrupt the process of blessing by interposing themselves to destroy faith and create doubt.

While there is abundant evidence for the promise and provision of divine blessing, there are also many blessing bandits. These can come in the form of satanic attack from powers that have aligned themselves against God and his children and seek to obviate or circumvent the covenantal faithfulness and contingent blessing of God in believers' lives. They can also be manifest as fellow humans who disparage or minimize the extent of one's gift of grace from God. Blessing bandits can also take the form of human self-doubts and feelings of inadequacy that limit faith in the ultimate fulfillment of divine promises. Any of these elements can result in the believer's loss of the blessing that God has intended.

In the story of the Abrahamic covenant and blessing, there is also a poignant demonstration of the kinds of attacks that are mounted against God's children in an effort to steal their blessing. When God came to Abraham and instructed him to slaughter various animals, halve their bodies, and lay the halves opposite their counterparts, he was engaging in the ancient custom of "cutting a covenant."[2] Both parties to such an agreement would walk between the halves of the animal carcasses, visually demonstrating that they would deserve a similar fate if they should violate the terms of their covenant.

In confirming his covenant with Abraham, God used the demonstration that was traditional to the culture of the time. After Abraham had laid out the animals' bodies on the ground according to the Lord's instructions,[3] he paused to see what God would do. As he waited, the patriarch immediately encountered forces that were focused on stealing the sacrifice and obviating the covenant of God's grace to his chosen servant. These forces took three forms that are described as being interposed between the command for sacrifice and the time that God spoke immutable fiery words of promise and blessing.

DRIVING THE VULTURES AWAY

The first of these bandits took the form of birds of prey or vultures that flocked around to steal the pieces of the sacrifice that served as a visual demonstration of the covenant and its attendant blessing. They attacked what Abraham had offered, seeking to consume his offering and thereby deny it to God. When the patriarch drove the vultures away, he established a clear example of the believer's constant need to guard what he has offered to God.

Of course, the scavengers do not always take the form of feathered fiends with shredding talons and ravenous beaks. Often they are other people who disparage the vision or the determination that one has for fulfilling God's will. Abraham and visionaries in later times who have dared to enter into face-to-face encounters with God have been questioned and disparaged by those who fight to maintain the *status quo*.[4] They have been judged inadequate, and their visions impossible.

When those whom God has challenged with responsibilities for change allow themselves to be picked apart by their detractors to the extent that they begin to doubt the validity of their vision, the pieces of their covenantal sacrifice are being stolen away. If they do not rise up immediately and take spiritual action against such bandits, they may be overcome and lose the benefits of God's benediction. The visual image of Abraham's driving the vultures away from his sacrifice should reinforce the believer's need to be vigilant and forceful in maintaining his own faith, while at the same taking an active role in driving away doubt.

OVERCOMING SOMNOLENCE

The second force that Abraham faced was the spirit of a deep sleep that seized him. If he had succumbed to this force, the vultures would have completely removed the sacrifice which represented the covenant. Satan and his emissaries are thoroughly skilled and equipped with somnolent agents, sleeping pills that can rapidly lull even the most passionate believer to sleep. If the enemy cannot steal the sacrifice outright, he will attempt to induce a soporific state, a complete relaxing of the guard.

When promised a blessing from God, one must be eternally vigilant, overcoming the spirit of slumber and standing secure in God's benediction. This is a part of the process of progressive salvation, in which one who has been saved positionally by grace through faith[5] in the completed work of atonement in Jesus Christ continues to "work out his own salvation with fear and trembling,"[6] so that he "endures to the end" and "is saved."[7] Faithfulness to endure to the time when the promise is to be fulfilled is essential to receiving the blessing that God has prepared. After one has "patiently endured," he obtains the promise in exactly the same manner that Abraham did 4,000 ago.[8]

DEALING WITH TERROR

The third challenge that Abraham experienced was the "horror of darkness." The forces of evil that sought to deny Abraham his covenantal blessing mounted an attack of horrific proportions. Abraham was, no doubt, reminded that because he was more than ninety years old and his wife Sarah was an octogenarian, God's promise of a child for them was impossible. Abraham faced the horror of sinking into the darkness of death without a legitimate heir. The terror of unfulfilled vision and expectation was overwhelming; however, God reassured the patriarch that he would die in peace at a good old age.[9]

The human feeling of inadequacy in the face of insurmountable challenge can generate a feeling of absolute terror in the heart of the most faith-filled believer. Often in the face of this attack one is like Jehoshaphat whose heart was filled with fear to such a degree that he confessed that he did not know what to do.[10] When those who are given a vision from God and the promise of a covenantal blessing that will impact countless others, they often stop to consider the seemingly insurmountable obstacles that confront them. When they do, they are seized with a very human fear. This kind of fear is merely the normal biological quality that prepares humans for fight or flight. It is an adrenaline rush of profound proportions, especially when one has no idea what to do in the face of terror's onslaught.

Jehoshaphat's strategy, however, always works in the face of such horrific attacks. He set himself to seek the Lord.[11] "Our eyes are on you," he declared,[12] reminding God of the prayer that his ancestor Solomon had prayed at the dedication of the temple[13] and of the Lord's response that he would hear the humble petitions of his people.[14]

God responded to Jehoshaphat's prayer with words of assurance: "This battle is not for you to fight . . . stand still and see the victory of the Lord on your behalf."[15]

In the face of the most horrible self-doubts, the believer must ever have his gaze fixed upon the Lord, knowing that every battle belongs to God. He will recognize that his help comes from above; therefore, he will not divert his attention from God to focus on the frightening circumstances around him. Rather than telling God how overwhelming his problems are, he will tell his problems how overwhelming his God is! Like Abraham he will realize that his future, like his past and his present, is in God's hand and that what God has promised will be fulfilled. God cannot lie, and he cannot fail. His promised blessings are immutable, because he is the Lord who changes not.[16]

SEEING THE FIRE OF BLESSING

After Abraham had endured the attack of these three forces, in due time he looked up and came face to face with the God who is the consuming fire.[17] The fire was a theophany, a literal appearance of God. A supernatural fiery torch passed between the two halves of Abraham's sacrifices, confirming the covenant that God had sealed with the patriarch and his progeny.[18] God then promised all the land from the Euphrates River to the river of Egypt to Abraham's descendants. By passing through the sacrifice, God, in effect, made an oath of blessing. To confirm the efficacy of his promise, God revealed himself for the first time as *El Shaddai*,[19] the Almighty, the all-sufficient one.

Only God passed between the pieces of the sacrifice, for the Abrahamic covenant was a unilateral covenant, not a bilateral agreement. It was contingent solely on God's covenantal faithfulness and was not based on Abraham's performance. The only thing that was required of Abraham was faith, and that faith was generated by God's Word to him. In like manner, the believer's status before God and

his worthiness of blessing is not contingent upon his performance of works of righteousness. They are based in faith
and in faith only. Statements of "I'm not worthy . . ." are
absurd! Of course, no one is worthy of God's favor. His grace
is wholly unmerited, a gift of God's love. Status before God
and worthiness for blessing are neither gained nor maintained
by works or by knowledge. God's blessing results solely from
faith and the faithfulness that is its outworking.

THE BLESSING IS SECURE

Those who maintain faith and faithfulness before God,
believing his promises, will realize the fulfillment of his
covenantal benefits in God's own time. God's blessing is
sure and secure. Nothing present or future,[20] visible or invisible can interdict or obviate God's benediction. Though
blessing bandits mass on horizons clouded with doubt, their
aggression and terrorism cannot consume the believer, for
he is enshrouded in God's presence and protection. Destruction can rain down upon neighbors all around; however, it will not come near the one who has placed himself
under the shadow of the Almighty.[21] The fire that is the
Lord will give light in the most abject darkness, it will give
security in the most horrific terror, and it will bring irrevocable blessing in the most damnable malediction. God
will keep those in perfect peace whose minds are fixed on
him.[22] God's blessing is secure.

[1] Hebrews 6:15.

[2] M. Weinfeld, "The Covenant of Grace in the Old Testament and
in the Ancient Near East," *Journal of the American Oriental Society*, 90
(1970), p. 184.

[3] Genesis 15:7-10.

[4] It has been said that *status quo* is a Latin phrase that means "the
mess we're in." No matter how horrible the existing condition, there
are always those who wish to maintain it all costs, relying on the maxim:
"Misery loves company."

[5] Ephesians 2:8.

[6] Philippians 2:12.

[7] Matthew 24:13; Mark 13:13.

[8] Hebrews 6:13-16.
[9] Genesis 15:15.
[10] 2 Chronicles 20:3, 12.
[11] 2 Chronicles 20:3.
[12] 2 Chronicles 20:12.
[13] 2 Chronicles 6:14-42.
[14] 2 Chronicles 7:12-18.
[15] 2 Chronicles 20:15, 17, NRSV.
[16] Malachi 3:6.
[17] Deuteronomy 4:24; Hebrews 12:29.
[18] Genesis 15:17.
[19] Before that time, God had been known as *El* or *Elohim.*
[20] Romans 8:38.
[21] Psalm 91:1, 7.
[22] Isaiah 26:3.

Chapter 11

Hands
of Blessing

One of the most unique practices in the ancient world was the "laying on of hands." In modern society, such an enigmatic act seems rather quaint. What possible significance could placing one's hands on another person have? Is such action merely symbolic, or does an actual physical exchange occur? What does the physical touch signify? Is this ancient symbol significant in today's world, and what role, if any, does it play in the transfer of blessing?

In biblical times the laying on of hands was an important function within the community of faith, both in the economy of Israel and in the time of the earliest church. This practice was of such significance that it is listed as one of six foundational principles of the teaching of Christ, right alongside repentance, faith, baptism, resurrection, and eternal judgment.[1] In such an outline of cardinal tenets of faith, laying on of hands seems an incongruity. Because the author used the term in this foundational context, however, it must have far-reaching significance.

HANDS FOR ANCIENT BLESSING

From antiquity, the laying on of hands, particularly the right hand, was used for a variety of reasons, including commissioning or ordination and the transfer of blessings.

Generational inheritance and blessing were conveyed by laying the right hand upon the one who was to receive the inheritance and blessing.

Before Isaac died, he was preparing to bless his firstborn son Esau; however, his wife, Rebecca, and her favored son, Jacob, conspired to have the blessing of inheritance placed upon Jacob. Esau had previously bartered away his inheritance and blessing to Jacob for the proverbial bowl of pottage. What had been the older son's entitlement through the ancient and enduring system of the right of primogenitor (the inheritance to the firstborn son) became Jacob's through his somewhat deceptive bartering.

In order to complete the transaction and actually receive the blessing and the inheritance, however, Jacob and his mother had to arrange to have Isaac lay his right hand upon Jacob and transfer the blessing. Since Isaac was advanced in age and was nearly blind, the task was much less difficult. All that was necessary was for the patriarch to be convinced that it was Esau who had come before him for the blessing. Rebecca, therefore, attached animal skins to Jacob's smooth arms so that they would feel like those of the rugged outdoorsman, Esau. Though Isaac was suspicious of Jacob's voice, he was convinced that it was Esau who was before him and laid his right hand upon him and blessed him.

Something spiritual and eternal occurred with the blessing that made it irreversible. Though Esau lamented the situation and even plotted the murder of his brother, there was nothing that Isaac could do to change what had been done. Jacob had been blessed, and he was the blessed one. This one truth should underscore the idea of the irrevocable nature and permanence of a blessing that is conveyed with divine authority and in divine order.

Decades later, when Jacob neared the end of his life, he gathered his own sons about him and pronounced a prophetic blessing upon them one by one, noting their qualities and predicting what they would accomplish and what would be their destinies.[2] The Scriptures relate this event very poignantly: "All these are the twelve tribes of Israel, and this is what their father said to them when he blessed them. He blessed them, every one with the blessing appropriate to him."[3]

Shortly before Jacob blessed his sons in this manner, he also blessed two of his grandsons, Manasseh and Ephraim, the sons of his beloved Joseph. When Joseph brought his sons before their grandfather for his blessing, he positioned them so that the elder, Manasseh, would have Jacob's right hand laid upon his head; however, Jacob was prophetically moved to cross his hands deliberately so that his right hand was upon the head of Ephraim instead. Even though Joseph implored his father to bless the elder as the custom was, he insisted on blessing the younger. The central role that the laying on of the right hand played in this blessing is significant. It underscores the importance that the significant touch of the right hand can have in any blessing process.

WHY THE RIGHT HAND?

Until modern times, the right hand was considered to be the hand of blessing, the good hand, as it were. This was true of many cultures, including those of biblical lands. It was the right hand that was used for eating; therefore, it was a focus of attention for cleanliness and purity. The left hand, on the other hand, was used for attending to bodily functions. To touch one with the right hand, then, was a blessing. To do so with the left hand was a sign of contempt.

In the more recent times, the residue of this ancient tradition remains, with language even emphasizing the basis of the tradition. The words *gauche* (awkward or uncoordinated) and *sinister* (ominous or threatening) were terms for "left handed" in their original languages (French and Latin), while the words *dexterous* (skillful or graceful) and *adroit* (clever) derive from Latin and Middle French terms for "right handed." Solomon confirmed this ongoing view: "A wise man's heart is at his right hand, but a fool's heart at his left."[4]

This is, no doubt, the reason for the continuing custom of extending the right hand in peace, the basis of the modern handshake. The extended open hand has been a clear sign of a lack of violent intentions, for one can see that no weapon is present. It is probable that this sign also emerged from the fact that a significant majority of the human population is right handed, with motor skills better developed in the right hand than in the left. More than this, however, the extended right hand is a sign of peace and blessing.

From the most ancient times, the order for the delegation of authority flowed first to the right hand. The king's prime minister was always his "right-hand man," a term that endures even to the present time to indicate the person of greatest importance to a leader. The second ruler in the kingdom sat at the king's right hand; therefore, this seat was generally reserved for the sovereign's firstborn son.

The right hand is the hand of authority. When God brings judgment upon the earth, he does so through his right hand.[5] In the giving of the Decalogue at Sinai, it was said that "from [God's] right hand went forth a fiery law for [Israel]."[6] It is recorded that Job understood that only the Lord's right hand could save.[7] David confirmed repeatedly the fact that salvation and blessing come from God's right hand.[8] Likewise, in God's kingdom, the emphasis of power is at the right hand.[9] The only begotten Son of God, Jesus, sits at the right hand of the father in heaven,[10] ever interceding for humankind. All power and dominion are given to the Son on the right hand.

Even in the process of anointing the priesthood of Israel, the emphasis was on the right hand. Moses took blood and placed it upon the tip of Aaron's right ear, upon the thumb of his right hand, and upon the great toe of his right foot.[11] The same thing was done by the priest for the worshiper who brought a trespass offering to the Lord: the blood of the sacrifice was placed upon his right ear, right thumb, and right great toe.[12] Likewise, the oil of blessing that was offered before the Lord was sprinkled seven times from the priest's right finger[13] and then was placed upon the worshiper's right ear, right thumb, and right great toe.

ORDINATION AND APPOINTMENT

When ancient leaders wished to set forth their (or God's) choice for their successors, they generally did so by a public act of demonstration that focused on the laying on of hands. Since the hand was seen as a symbol of strength and power, the laying on of hands was a way of extending power and authority. Moses "took Joshua, and set him . . . before all the congregation. Then he laid his hands upon him and commissioned him."[14] Apparently this act involved the transfer of authority and anointing, for later it was observed that "Joshua . . . was filled with the spirit of wisdom *because Moses had laid his hands on him*"[15] (emphasis added).

In matters of ordination or appointment of leaders to offices within the church, laying hands on the ordainee was central to the process. When Paul and Barnabas were to be commissioned for ministry to the Gentiles, they were ordained by the apostles: "James and Cephas and John . . . gave to me and Barnabas the right hands of fellowship, that we should go unto the Gentiles. . . ."[16]

This procedure was likely used in the ordination of elders in the various assemblies of the church.[17] Elders were ordained in every city by being set before the people and "before the Lord."[18] This practice was not original to the nascent church. It was borrowed from the rich tradition of the Jewish people of whom they were inherently a part. Those who were recognized as teachers in the communities of Israel were appointed by the laying on of hands. This physical act was a demonstration of community recognition of authority and divine calling.[19]

Even in the case of direct divine appointment, the laying on of hands is significant. When the apostle John received his commission to write the apocalyptic vision that he was experiencing on the Isle of Patmos, he reported that the glorified Son of Man whom he had just seen in the midst of seven golden lampstands "laid his right hand on me, saying . . . write, therefore, what you have seen, what is now and what will take place later."[20] The very last revelatory experience in Holy Scripture was accompanied by the laying on of hands, in this case the right hand of the Lord himself.

TRANSFER OF ANOINTING AND POWER

The idea of the transfer of spiritual anointing through the laying on of hands continued into the earliest church, where it was observed that the apostles had the unique gift of imparting the Holy Spirit to believers through this means. When word was received in Jerusalem that believers in Samaria had accepted the good news of salvation through Jesus, the apostles dispatched Peter and John thence. They "prayed for them that they might receive the Holy Spirit. . . . Then they laid hands on them, and they received the Holy Spirit."[21] This act was so profound that Simon the sorcerer offered money to Peter and John, imploring them, "Give me also this ability so that everyone on whom I lay my hands may receive the Holy Spirit."[22] Peter declared, "What I have, I give to you,"[23] as he took the paralytic by the right hand and lifted him up healed.

Much later, Paul encouraged Timothy to rekindle the gift that God had given him when the apostle and the elders of the assembly had laid their hands on him: "I remind you to fan into flame the gift of God, which is in you through the laying on of my hands."[24] Paul had previously clarified to Timothy the nature of this impartation in another exhortation: "Do not neglect the gift that is in you, which was given to you by prophecy with the laying on of the hands of the eldership."[25]

Precisely what is involved in the exchange of anointing

or blessing by means of the laying on of hands is not clear. In various cases in Jesus' ministry, those whom he touched and those who touched him experienced the transfer of "power," the means by which they were healed or delivered from various maladies.[26] It has been medically proven that the human touch has therapeutic value to those who are ill. It has also been empirically demonstrated that those for whom prayers are offered, whether in person or from a distance, heal more quickly than those who are not the object of prayer. While it is difficult to comprehend this exchange of power, it is, nevertheless, a fact of both Scripture and science. The laying on of hands is actually more than a mere formality.

BLESSING HANDS

If the laying on of hands was of such significance that it was employed in the ordination of prophets, kings, and leaders of faith communities, it certainly has significance in the process of blessing. Though it may sound strange, a spiritual transfer of authority, ability, or blessing occurs through the agency of the human touch. Philosopher David Spangler says, "A blessing is the passing of spirit between [people]."[27] This is the reason for the ongoing practice that continues to this day in Jewish households when parents place their hands on the heads of their children while blessing them with the Aaronic benediction. "Blessing is increase in strength and life; blessing is success and expansion; blessing is the dynamic of life."[28]

It should come as no surprise, then, that Jesus himself used this same Hebraic methodology in his interaction with children. Since Jesus was in every way a proper, Torah-observant Jew who was fully integrated into the culture and traditions of Second Temple Judaism, it was only natural that when children were brought to him, "he took them up in his arms, put his hands on them, and blessed them."[29] Jesus was merely continuing a two-millennia old Jewish tradition of blessing.

This and other similar actions are more than ceremonial: they actually make an impartation. Though it may seem quaint to modern society, the Word of God actually works. What God has commissioned is efficacious, and those whom he has assigned responsibility to bless are empowered to convey the blessing both by word and deed. This power has not been reserved exclusively to the clergy. All believers share the priesthood, just as all ministers are laity. All believers, therefore, are empowered to bless according to the grace of God that is given to them. As believers assume their God-given anointing to bless, they will flow freely in the "doctrine of the laying on of hands" and will find that blessing flows from their mouths and from their hands into the lives of others.

[1] Hebrews 6:1-2.
[2] Genesis 49:2-33.
[3] Genesis 49:28, NASB.
[4] Ecclesiastes 10:2.
[5] Exodus 15:12.
[6] Deuteronomy 33:2.
[7] Job 40:14.
[8] Psalm17:7; 20:6; 44:3; 98:1; 108:6; 138:7;
[9] Psalm 110:1.
[10] Acts 7:56; Hebrews 8:1; 10:12; 12:2.
[11] Leviticus 8:23.
[12] Leviticus 14:14.
[13] Leviticus 14:16.
[14] Numbers 27:22, NKJV; 27:23, NIV.
[15] Deuteronomy 34:9, NIV.
[16] Galatians 2:9, ASV.
[17] Titus 1:5.
[18] Acts 14:23.
[19] Timothy N. Boyd, "The Laying on of Hands," *Biblical Illustrator* 15 (1989), p. 10.
[20] Revelation 1:17, KJV; 1:19, NIV.
[21] Acts 8:15, NIV; 8:17, NKJV.
[22] Acts 8:19, NIV.
[23] Acts 3:6-7, NIV.
[24] 2 Timothy 1:6, NIV.
[25] 1 Timothy 4:14.
[26] Mark 5:30; Luke 6:19; 8:46.
[27] David Spangler, *Blessing: The Art and the Practice* (New York: Riverhead, 2001), p. 48.
[28] F. Hurst, quoted in Renner, " 'Believing' in the Beginning of Blessing-History," p. 50.
[29] Mark 10:16.

Chapter 12

Releasing God to Bless

What one receives in the way of gain through the works of his hands is the substance of continued life. The believer in the God of Israel understands that all that he acquires is the gift of God's grace and is not the product of his own acumen or physical prowess. God is man's source. God's will is that all men should be blessed beyond all measure of their own expectations. In order for God to bless, however, the believer must recognize and demonstrate his understanding that he is completely dependent upon God's provision for his sustenance. The medium of this demonstration is the gain that man achieves through the work of his hands.

The patriarch Abraham demonstrated this process when he approached God's priest, Melchizedek, with his tithes, one-tenth of his gain, as an offering to the Lord. Abraham's success and the profit that he had made were not the product of his own genius or of his physical strength. They were the result of God's blessing and the bounty of God's provision. The patriarch's act of tithing his increase set the example of faith for all his descendants, both natural and spiritual.

From the earliest days of the Israelite nation, God instructed the people to tithe the produce of their agrarian enterprise. If they could not do so, they were to turn their gain into money and to bring a tenth of that money to the priests as an offering to the Lord.[1] Money is the means for providing the elements needed to support life. As such, money is good and a blessing from God. The love of money, however, is the root of all evil[2] because the passion to accumulate resources with no consideration for God or man is an expression of self-sufficiency and independence from God. What one does with money is a clear indication of the attitude of one's heart, "for where your treasure is, there will your heart be also."[3] This is especially true of the tithe.

TEN PERCENT OR ONE HUNDRED PERCENT?

God has so designed it that when one tithes his gain, the Eternal accepts that tenth as though it were the whole. The word for tithe, *mesher*, means both "a tenth" and "a very large amount, abundance, or wealth." In effect, the giving of the tenth to God is a demonstration that one has given his entire gain to God. It is a statement that one is not grasping what he has gained, thinking that his own ability has provided for his continuing sustenance. He is giving back to God because he believes that everything he possesses has been given to him by God. There is no hint of self-sufficiency.

The act of tithing is a mechanism that releases God to bless. God himself lays down the axiom of this process: "Bring the whole tithe into the storehouse. . . . Test me in this . . . and see if I will not throw open the floodgates of heaven and pour out so much blessing that you will not have room enough for it."[4] God promises that if one fully tithes his gain into God's treasury, the floodgates of heaven will open with an uncontainable blessing. What a profound promise!

A DECLARATION

The tenth of increase was considered to be holy or separated unto the Lord.[5] Upon entering the land of promise, Israel was commanded to bring the firstfruits of its harvests (the tithe) to the Lord. The priests were to place those firstfruits in a basket and present them before the Lord in his sanctuary. The worshiper was to confess before the Lord that his father was a wandering Aramean who sojourned in Egypt where bondage awaited his descendants. God, however, was faithful to deliver them and to bring them into a land flowing with milk and honey. The tithe was a demonstration that God himself was the Israelite's provider.

When one had fully tithed and confessed his heritage of inclusion in the Abrahamic covenant, he was to attest that he had taken the hallowed things (the tithes) out of his house and had brought them to the priesthood, thereby fulfilling God's commandment. Once he had made this affirmation, he was permitted to pray this petition for blessing: "Look down from heaven, your holy dwelling place, and bless your people Israel and the land you have given us."[6] The declaration of blessing was then placed upon the worshiper: "You have declared this day that the Lord is your God and that you will walk in his ways. . . . The Lord has declared this day that you are his people, his treasured possession."[7] Because the believer had brought his treasure to God, he was declared to be God's treasure! God was assured that his people had affirmed him as their God when they brought their tithe to his sanctuary. Because of their faithfulness to demonstrate their dependence upon him, God declared that he would exalt them. What a blessing!

As this story of the importance, nature, and system of tithing was completed, God promised, "And all these blessings shall come upon you and overtake you, because you obey the voice of the Lord your God: The Lord will command the blessing on you . . . in all to which you set your hand. The Lord will open the heavens, the storehouse of his bounty."[8] The language here is what the promise of Malachi mirrors: the windows of heaven will be open with incomprehensible blessing to those who demonstrate their dependence and faithfulness to God through the act of tithing. The act of tithing is the one sure means of proving God and ensuring his blessing, for God will "command" the blessing and release his bounty.

Malachi spoke of both tithes and offerings as a means of releasing God to bless. This underscores the fact that God expects more than the tenth. The tithe is man's responsibility to God; however, the offering is man's free will love gift to God and others. Giving is more a measure of one's dependence upon God than the tithe. One can be parsimonious and legalistically exact the tithe; however, the offering is an open expression of the heart and is evidence of one's generosity that courts God's favor in the blessing that is shaken down, pressed together, and running over.[9] Tithing can be legalistic; offering is ever faith and love based.

TZEDAKAH AND THE GOOD EYE

A major function of the practice of tithing in the Hebrew Scriptures was to support the priesthood and the sanctuary cultus; however, from earliest times, a significant part of giving was for assisting the poor, the widows, and the orphans of society. This part of the giving of the Israelites and of the Jewish people in succeeding generations was considered of such importance that it came to be called *tzedakah*, the Hebrew word for righteousness.

This fact underscores a significant difference between Jewish and Christian approaches to assisting the less fortunate in society. Christian giving to the needy has always been looked upon as charity, giving that is born out of compassion or pity for the suffering. A Christian gives to others because of philanthropic impulses in what is more often than not an emotional response to need. If the situation or circumstance is not sufficiently heart-rending, there is often little giving.

Jewish giving, on the other hand, is based on God's

command that a significant portion of income be set aside to be given to those in need.[10] To give to the poor or suffering is doing a *mitzvah*, fulfilling a commandment. There is no need for an emotional appeal to open the purse strings. Among the Jews, giving is a given! Great analyses have been presented in the Jewish community as to the motives and methods of giving. The highest and best is for one to give to another in such a way that the giver does not know the recipient and the beneficiary does not know the benefactor.

Solomon declared, "He who has a generous eye will be blessed, for he gives of his bread to the poor."[11] Literally, this text says, "He who has a good [*tov*] eye will be blessed." This is also the meaning of Jesus' statement: "The eye is the lamp of the body. If your eyes are good, your whole body will be full of light."[12] The Master's declaration was made in the context of the these observations: "Where your treasure is, there will your heart be also" (the pretext), and, "You cannot serve God and mammon" (the subtext). Responding to God's commandment to give to others with generosity underscores man's dependence upon God's provision and not upon his own prowess. It also recognizes the fact that all people are God's children and that all life is sacred and worthy of support. If one has a good eye of generosity, his entire being is filled with the light of life. Indeed, doing "good works" is the way in which the light of the world is manifest and God is glorified.[13]

When one is generous, his visual acuity is heightened so that he can see more clearly the light of God's presence and respond to the illumination of his Word. This opens the way for the impartation of God's blessing according to the divine law of reciprocity: one receives in kind what he sows and in direct proportion to the amount he sows. "Give, and it will be given to you . . . for with the measure you sow, it will be measured to you."[14] Since God "loves a cheerful giver,"[15] he responds to those who share their resources with others, and he showers them with multiple blessings.

DESIRES OF THE HEART

Obeying God's commandment for tithing and giving is one clear signal of submission to divine imperatives in other areas of life. Such obedience is foundational to receiving God's blessing, for God can never bless that which he does not approve. King David succinctly described this divine law: "Delight yourself in the Lord; and he will give you the desires of your heart. Commit your way to the Lord, trust also in him, and he will do it."[16] Delighting in the Lord is not some warm, fuzzy, emotional feeling. It is delighting in the instructions and commandments of the Lord.[17]

Jesus emphasized the importance of obedience in the process of blessing: "You may ask me for anything in my name, and I will do it. If you love me, you will obey what I command."[18] Often believers have thought that loving Jesus exempted them from obedience to divine commandments; however, the truth is that there is no evidence of love for God if one does not manifest obedience to God's commandments.

John reestablished for the church the truth that blessings result from obedience: "[We] receive from him anything we ask, because we obey his commands and do what pleases him."[19] The apostle even asserted that the only evidence that confirms true relationship with God is faithfulness to fulfill God's commandments: "The man who says, 'I know him,' but does not do what he commands is a liar, and the truth is not in him."[20] The morbid fear that some Christians have of the commandments of Scripture, thinking that obedience to God's instructions is "legalism" and "bondage," is not substantiated in the teachings of Jesus or of John.

The blessings of God are secure unto those who fulfill

the instructions of his Word. As a matter of fact, God himself has assured believers that when they are obedient to his
commands, divine blessings will "overtake" them: "Now it
shall be, if you will diligently obey the Lord your God,
being careful to do all his commandments . . . all these blessings shall come upon you and overtake you, if you obey
the Lord your God."[21] The blessings of God are inescap-
able for those who love God and demonstrate their love
as Abraham did through faithfulness to God's will and
Word. When believers love God and are obedient, blessings will overtake them so that they will be blessed in
everything that they do.

Receiving blessing from God, then, is not the result
of understanding magic formulae or reciting specially prepared incantations. Blessing is assured through obedience
to the divine instructions that God has given for his people,
the most easily demonstrable of which is the commandment for tithing and giving.

Paving the Way of Blessing

Tithing and giving, then, are the scriptural means of
preparing a highway for a convoy of blessings. Those who
are obedient to God's commandments in regard to money
and other resources discover that they release God to bless
all the works of their hands. They do not wait for some
tragic circumstance to tug at their heart strings. In true
Hebraic tradition, they give systematically and continually
because they love God and because they love their fellow
man. They know that both Jesus and Paul described this
kind of love as equivalent to fulfilling the entire corpus of
God's law.[22] Their generosity causes their entire human experience to be filled with the divine light. It is the key to the
strongbox of God's treasure, and it is divine insurance that
the richest of God's blessings will always belong to them.

[1] Deuteronomy 14:28.
[2] 1 Timothy 6:10.

[3] Matthew 6:21.
[4] Malachi 3:10, NIV.
[5] Leviticus 27:30.
[6] Deuteronomy 26:15, NIV.
[7] Deuteronomy 26:17-18, NIV.
[8] Deuteronomy 28:2, NKJV; 28:12, NIV.
[9] Luke 6:38.
[10] Exodus 23:11; Deuteronomy 15:7.
[11] Proverbs 22:9.
[12] Matthew 6:22, NIV.
[13] Matthew 5:16.
[14] Luke 6:38, NIV.
[15] 2 Corinthians 9:7.
[16] Psalm 37:4-5, NASB.
[17] Psalm 1:2.
[18] John 14:14-15, NIV.
[19] 1 John 3:22, NIV.
[20] 1 John 2:4, NIV.
[21] Deuteronomy 28:1-2, NASB.
[22] Mark 12:30-31, Romans 13:10.

Chapter 13

The Blessing of Blessing What God Has Blessed

In order to ensure God's blessing and at the same time avoid God's curse, it is important that one learn the lesson of blessing what God has blessed. This important truth is established in the blessing that God gave to Abraham in the beginning of his covenant relationship with his chosen people.

"I will bless them that bless you, and I will curse him that curses you," God promised Abraham."[1] God made an everlasting covenant with Abraham that would ensure the blessing that he had given to the patriarch would flow generationally to his descendants after him. Along with God's blessing upon Abraham and his progeny was a parallel blessing upon those who would bless them and a curse upon anyone who would dare to curse them.

Imbedded in the Abrahamic covenant, therefore, is a blessing that anyone can receive. The only precondition for receiving God's blessing is that one bless the descendants of Abraham. The chosen people of history and of the present are a touchstone of blessing. Those who bless the Hebrews, the Israelites, and the Jews are destined to receive blessing from the God of Abraham, Isaac, and Jacob. Individuals, communities, and nations can all benefit from this blessing both materially and spiritually. "I will bless those who bless my people," the God of heaven continues to say just as he did four millennia ago.

A CURSE UPON THE CURSER

At the same time, however, a curse is certain to be delivered upon those who curse God's chosen people. "I will curse him that curses you," God continues to say. As a result of this ancient commitment, individuals, communities, and nations open themselves to God's curse when they choose to curse the people whom God has blessed. Indeed, the land-scape of history is littered with the carcasses of people and nations who have dared to raise up their hands against the linear descendants of Abraham, Isaac, and Jacob.

One would think that peoples would learn the lesson of history; however, they remain blinded by the god of this world who thinks to overthrow the blessing that God has established. Time and again, they arrogantly spew forth their imprecations, mount their physical attacks, and seek to undo what God has done. Time and again, they find that the curse that they invent returns to them with devastation.

A clear lesson of this divine truth was seen in the case of Balaam when he sought to enrich himself by cursing Israel on behalf of Balak, the Moabite king.[2] Ultimately, the curses he had devised came forth from his mouth as blessings for Israel. "I cannot curse what God has blessed," he groaned to the furious king.

The divine principle of blessing what God has blessed continues to this day. Those nations that bless and support the international Jewish community and the nation of Israel ensure for themselves the continuation of divine blessings. On the other hand, those nations that support anti-Semitism and anti-Zionism ensure for themselves the ongoing curse of God. And though many may laugh in the face of God because his tender mercies delay the execution of his judgment, God's curse is as certain as his blessing. The bones of today's anti-Semites will join in the ossuaries of history the accumulated remains of those nations that have cursed God's chosen people.

TURNING A CURSE INTO A BLESSING

Ultimately, what men of evil have meant for curses will result in blessing when those curses are directed against God's chosen. God will always have the final word, and his word is one of blessing. Whenever determined evil men–or even misguided good men, for that matter–direct curses against God's anointed ones, the Lord of heaven will see that what they have designed to be a curse will ultimately be a blessing that will benefit both the one who has been cursed and even those who have spoken the curse.

This was the case with Joseph, whose brothers' intention to kill him was mollified into their decision to sell him into slavery. What they had meant for evil, however, God meant for good.[3] God turned the evil act of Joseph's brothers into an ultimate blessing for him and for his family as he used their calumny to position his servant for ascension to the role of Egypt's prime minister, a position in which he was able to save his entire family from a seven-year famine that would have decimated them.

AVOIDING THE CURSE

People should exercise great care in imposing curses and judgmental words upon others. One never knows when he is engaging in this kind of action whether he is cursing what God has cursed or is cursing what God has blessed, for no one is omniscient and able to discern the heart as God does. Indeed, it may be better for everyone who is a believer in the God of Israel not to engage in cursing at all. The ultimate judgment of all men is in God's hands; therefore, humans should leave judgment to the One who is qualified to exact it.

Evil and judgmental words that are spoken over others can return to haunt the one who has spoken them, for with whatever measure one judges another, he will be judged in the same manner.[4] It is easy to be caught up in the self-righteous spirit of judgmentalism. It is also easy to speak judgments and curses against what is perceived as being manifestly evil; however, if God did not send his Son into the world to condemn the world but to save,[5] he has certainly not commissioned the church to do so. It is the role only of the Holy Spirit to convict the world of sin and bring God's judgment. [6]

It behooves believers, therefore, always to be bearers of the "good news." The gospel is the power of God unto salvation, not unto judgment and curse.[7] When the church has enshrouded itself in robes of judgment and has ensconced itself in forensic tribunals, it has totally missed its mark and calling. The resulting Christian triumphalism has negatively impacted both the church and its mission in the world. It is an unending truth that out of the same fountain cannot come good and bitter waters, blessing and curses.[8]

ENSURING GOD'S BLESSING

It is important for believers today who want to reap the benefits of God's blessing in their lives to remember to bless the people whom God has blessed. Endless opportunities for blessing the international Jewish community and the nation of Israel await the manifestation of simple acts of kindness and love. One might even find himself receiving the ultimate blessing of God when he is invited to assemble at the right hand of the heavenly throne. "Inasmuch as you did it to one of the least of these my brethren, you did it to me," the Lord will say.[9] And, could it be that the Messiah's brethren might just be his family according to the flesh, the Jewish people?

[1] Genesis 12:3.
[2] Numbers 22ff.
[3] Genesis 50:20.
[4] Luke 6:38.
[5] John 3:17.
[6] John 16:8.
[7] Romans 1:16.
[8] James 3:10-11.
[9] Matthew 25:40.

Chapter 14

Contending for Blessing

From a Hebraic perspective, prayer is more an action of conforming oneself to God's will than a means of inducing God to fulfill man's desires. It is an exercise in submitting to God's design, not an on-demand valet service. God is the source of man's unknown and unperceived need (which is often contrary to what man thinks he needs), and prayer is the means of communicating to God man's willingness to receive what God knows is needed. God is definitely not the great genie in the sky anxiously awaiting someone to stroke his bottle.

It is for this reason that most Jewish prayer is offered in the first person plural. Virtually all of the prayers in the *Siddur*[1] are corporate prayers. Indeed, some can be prayed only when a quorum of ten are present to offer the petition collectively. This is, no doubt, the reason that the prayer Jesus taught his disciples is prayed entirely in the first person plural: "*Our* Father . . . give *us* . . . forgive *us* . . . lead *us* . . . deliver *us*. . . ."[2] When one prays in a corporate sense, he sees the bigger picture and is not consumed with his own petty wants and wishes. He is not bogged down in consumerism prayer, the petition that is amiss because one seeks to secure God's favor on his own desires for pleasure.[3]

While the focus of Hebrew prayer is conformity

to God's will and seeking the good of community, still it maintains a place for individual petition. This is a manifestation of the traditional balance of Jewish thought that is able to hold seemingly opposing ideas in dynamic tension so that on the one hand there is truth, while on the other hand truth is also manifest. The synagogue liturgy that has focused on corporate petition has always had space for individual and personal prayer.

RECONFIRMING THE BLESSING

God's blessing is upon all the children of Abraham. This is a simple and undeniable truth. God swore[4] that he would fulfill his covenant with Abraham's children throughout all their generations forever.[5] While Abraham knew that the blessing was secure from the first moment that God spoke it, he frequently approached God for reconfirmation of that blessing. As he and his wife aged, he turned to God in personal angst that their expectations for an heir had not been realized. God did not rebuke him for "unbelief." Instead, he embraced him in his grace and reiterated the covenant and the promise.

Later Abraham's grandson, Jacob, wrestled with his own fears that the promise that had been given to his grandfather would fail in his, the third generation. He feared that his brother would have him assassinated. He had heard God reconfirm the covenant and the promise as he viewed the angelic hosts traversing a ladder from the heavenlies to earth, but, being human, he felt the need for a personal encounter with God and for a fresh impartation of personal blessing. Jacob had lived under the cloud of being a supplanter[6] who had received Isaac's birthright through deception. He needed reassurance that he truly was God's choice in the matter of inheritance and blessing. The one who had received the spectacular vision of heaven now needed an earthly encounter.

When Jacob came to the point of crossing the Jabbok, he knew that his life would change dramatically and there was a distinct possibility that he himself would not survive. It was during this night of decision that he "wrestled with the Lord." Perhaps Jacob joined with the Lord in contending with Jacob himself, for he needed divine assistance in overcoming himself. Whatever the case may have been, Jacob contended for the blessing and would not release the "angel" until he had received the divine blessing: "I will not let you go until you bless me."[7] His determination to contend for the blessing resulted in a new identity of blessing: thereafter the supplanter Jacob was called "Israel," a prince with God.

This is a clear paradigm for prevailing prayer where one wrestles with himself and with God in the face of deep-seated need. God will never reject one who engages him with such passion and intensity, with such *kavanah* (concentration and focus). Though the encounter with the Divine may leave one handicapped in some area of his life, it will ever galvanize his resolve to believe God and walk in the faith of realized promise. After Jacob's interaction with God, he walked ever thereafter with a limp, the evidence that he had engaged the Divine; however, he also walked in confidence that what God had promised, he would do.

But, this face-to-face encounter with God was not the end of God's blessing for Jacob. Some time later when he returned to Bethel, the place of his original vision, God appeared to him and "blessed him," repeating the promises that he had made to his grandfather, Abraham. The covenant and the blessing were reiterated, reestablished, and reconfirmed. God was ever present to reassure the patriarch of his support in each situation of life that he encountered.

Believers today, like Jacob of old, often need a reconfirmation of God's promise and blessing. This is not a manifestation of unbelief. It is simply a human need to be reassured in the face of a new encounter or a new challenge. Life is a series of such incidents where one faces the threatening and the unknown. Though one knows he is in covenant with God, he needs a reconfirmation of the blessing from God who is the Eternal and is ever present.

If God visited Abraham and Jacob repeatedly to reconfirm his covenant and blessing for them, he will do the same for all of his children. Abraham was blessed before he left Haran; he was blessed after Ishmael was born; he was blessed after the binding of Isaac; and when all was said and done, God "had blessed Abraham in all things."[8] Abraham's life was an unfolding of continuous blessing. When he was at his lowest ebb, God came to him to reconfirm the blessing. And God will do the same for all of Abraham's children who come to him for reassurance and confirmation.

BLESSING THROUGH PRAYER

It is proper for individuals to approach the Heavenly Father as his children, seeking his favor and the impartation of his blessing. A prominent example is recorded in the Psalms where David offered this form of the Aaronic benediction as a petition for blessing: "God be merciful unto us, and bless us, and cause his face to shine upon us."[9] This was a petition, a prayer invoking the divine presence to bless by turning his face toward his people. The petitionary blessing was offered continually to remind the people that God's blessing was ever with them. This benediction has been a song in Israel ever since David's time, for the Psalms were and remain the Jews' hymnal as well as the source of many of their prayers.

Another example of petitionary blessing is found in the prayer blessing of Jabez. A rather obscure character in Scripture, Jabez offered these words of petition: "O that you would bless me indeed and enlarge my border, and that your hand might be with me, and that you would keep me from harm that it may not pain me!"[10] In this case Jabez requested a personal blessing for himself, exclaiming his hope that God would bless him by bringing both physical and spiritual benefits to him. First he hoped that God would expand the range of his resources. Then he prayed that God would keep him from suffering. Is this not the very center of petition in the Lord's Prayer: "Give us this day our daily bread . . . and deliver us from evil"?

Is a blessing petition not a bit audacious? Would God countenance a such a petition of self-blessing and grant it? The answer is found in Scripture itself: "God granted [Jabez] what he requested." The boldness of Jabez' request maintained the continuing posture of the Hebrew people toward God. They came into his presence with "reverent boldness" (though the term might seem to be an oxymoron). While the Hebrew people had the highest respect for the honor of God the King, they also viewed him as their Father, one who would welcome them into his presence as a father would open his arms to his children. Indeed, one of the ancient Jewish prayers still prayed in today's synagogues begins, "*Avinu, Malkenu*" ("Our Father, our King").

The Bible recounts several instances where leaders of Israel had the *chutzpah* to engage God in dialogue and even to argue with him. Such was the case of Abraham who negotiated with God over the destiny of Sodom and Gomorrah.[11] Likewise Moses argued with God over the fate of the rebellious Israelites, even requesting that if God were settled on destroying Israel, he would destroy the prophet first.[12] Very often, petition has been seen as struggling with God, as when Jacob wrestled with God at Peniel.[13]

A great synagogue prayer known as the *Ne'ilah* declares: "Thou hast from the beginning set man apart, and made him worthy to stand before thee." In the context of this declaration, Abraham Joshua Heschel said that in prayer human beings "entrust themselves to him to whom their being and existence belong; they take a definitive position, spring up to make a claim before God, make a declaration, confess, pledge their souls, take possession, and enter into a covenant."[14]

Jesus himself underscored the nature of prayer in the illustration of the widow and the unjust judge, noting that the judge granted the widow's petition because she inconvenienced him. The Master concluded that if such an unjust jurist would answer the unrelenting petition of his subject, how much more would the Just Judge grant the prayers of his children.[15] This is why the writer of Hebrews urges all believers to "come boldly unto the throne of grace, that we may obtain mercy, and find grace to help in time of need."[16] The word *boldly* is παρρεσία (*parresia*) in Greek and means "frankly, without ambiguity or circumlocution, with fearless confidence." There is, therefore, no hint of timidity or reserve that should be exercised when approaching "the throne of grace," the seat of divine authority, to petition God for the blessing of his grace and mercy. One can have both humility and boldness in petitioning the Almighty.

SELF-BLESSING?

Is it possible for one to bless himself? The very idea sounds outrageous; however, there is one passage of Holy Scripture that makes this suggestion. In comparing the blessing of God upon those who are obedient to his Word with the curse that is upon the disobedient, God himself says prophetically that the time will come when "whoever blesses himself in the land shall bless himself by the true God."[17] The use of the Hebrew *hithpael* verb form is reflexive and is rightly translated, "blesses himself." Apparently God recognizes and honors self-blessings that are based in blessing by the true God or by the truth of God. Perhaps this was the underlying nature of the exercises of both David and Jabez when they exclaimed in God's presence, "Bless us!"

Blessing oneself is not merely the mindless repetition of religious words and phrases. It is the exercise of pure faith in the words of the living God. Jesus promised his disciples, "Everything you ask or pray for, believe that you have it already, and it will be yours."[18] The key is to bless oneself by the God of truth, so conforming one's desires to the will of God that what one seeks is what God already wants for him. Even though asking a blessing upon oneself may seem self-serving and void of humility, it is in reality a demonstration of dependence upon God and of faith in him and his Word. As Jesus promised, when one seeks God's kingdom first, all the material benefits that God has prepared for his servants will be added to them.[19]

One who blesses himself through petition must be careful that he is blessing himself in God and his truth. To do otherwise is to invite disaster and perhaps even curse. Because the heart of man is deceitful,[20] one must be careful with self-blessings, for they can be exercised through the imagination of the heart in defiance of God's manifest will.[21] When the heart is clearly in continuity with the Word and will of God, however, blessing oneself through petition for favor is honorable and pleasing to God.

PRAYING GOD'S WORD

One of the greatest secrets to successful prayer is praying God's Word. One cannot pray amiss when he prays the Word, for God's Word is infallible. The Jewish people have long understood this secret as evidenced by the fact that virtually all of their corporate prayers and affirmations are either quoted or paraphrased Holy Scripture.

It has been suggested that God, like men, enjoys hearing the sound of his own voice, particularly when that voice takes the form of the declaration of his Word from the lips of men.[22] The Word of God forms in the believer's heart the faith that is the substance of what is not apparent.[23] One can be sure that he is not praying words of selfish lust when he prays the words of Holy Scripture. That Word is alive and powerful.[24] It is active and generative. It changes the heart of the one through whom it is passing, and it opens that heart to receive the blessing that God intends, although not necessarily the ones that he imagines.

Christians could well profit from studying a *Siddur* just to see the beauty of the living words of God that are outlined in prayers. Perhaps a Christian *Siddur* should be created with an outline of Bible prayers that include those of the Apostolic Scriptures. At the very least, believers should begin to read the Bible with a view toward those prayers that were prayed and answered so that they can offer similar prayers and achieve similar results.

Praying God's Word is yet another part of the Christian's Hebraic heritage, that enriching connection with the book, the history, and the culture of God's chosen people. What great blessing awaits those who dare to be reconnected to the root system[25] of God's family tree of salvation and covenant relationship (the olive tree)!

PETITIONING FOR BLESSING

Jesus also made it clear that if a child of the kingdom asks the Heavenly Father for bread, he will not be given a stone.[26] If he asks for fish, he will not be given a serpent. Anyone who comes to God must believe that God exists and that he is a rewarder of those who diligently seek him.[27] One knows this for certain because Jesus Christ is the same yesterday, today, and forever.[28] The believer has an advocate with the Father who is touched with his deepest need.[29] Jesus will never drive away anyone who comes to him in faith.[30] He is always filled with compassion, and he stretches forth his hand of blessing to those who approach him in faith.

The boldness to petition God for blessing upon oneself is well within the entitlements of believers; however, they often have not because they ask not or because they ask amiss.[31] They must understand clearly that they always have access to the throne of God through Jesus Christ and the completed work of Calvary. With this right of entrance into the heavenlies through prayer, believers can position themselves before the throne of grace and receive the impartation of blessing into their lives even as they speak that blessing in words of faith in God's provision.

Just as little Jewish children are taught to seek out their parents with heads bowed for the impartation of the divine blessing, so believers should come boldly, yet reverently into their Father's presence expecting and receiving the reconfirmation of his promise and blessing. He will welcome them with open arms, place his hand upon them, and speak his everlasting benediction into their lives. When they contend for the blessing, they can be certain that he will give it to them in inconceivable dimensions. They already have his assurance that they need only ask, and they will receive.[32] It's really that simple!

[1] The Jewish prayer book is called a *Siddur*, from the word *seder*, meaning to set in order. It is a systematic approach to prayer that has been developed and refined over the past two millennia.

[2] Matthew 6:19.

[3] James 4:3.

[4] Hebrews 6:13.

[5] Genesis 17:7.

[6] Jacob's name even meant supplanter (Genesis 37:26).

[7] Genesis 32:26, NIV.

[8] Genesis 24:1.

[9] Psalm 67:1, ASV.

[10] 1 Chronicles 4:10, NASB.

[11] Genesis 18:22.

[12] Exodus 32:9-14; Deuteronomy 9:23-27; 10:10.

[13] Genesis 32:26.

[14] Abraham Heschel, quoted in di Sante, *Jewish Prayer*, p. ix.

[15] Luke 18:16.

[16] Hebrews 4:16, KJV.
[17] Isaiah 65:16, TNK.
[18] Mark 11:24, NJB.
[19] Matthew 6:33; Luke 12:31.
[20] Jeremiah 17:9.
[21] Deuteronomy 29:19.
[22] This idea was first expressed to me by Dawn Rawson.
[23] Hebrews 11:1.
[24] Hebrews 4:12.
[25] Romans 11:17.
[26] Matthew 7:9.
[27] Hebrews 11:6.
[28] Hebrews 13:8.
[29] 1 John 2:1; Hebrews 4:15.
[30] John 6:37.
[31] James 4:3.
[32] Luke 11:9.

Chapter 15

Family
Blessings

A significant part of God's blessing for Abraham was this declaration: "In you all the families of the earth shall be blessed."[1] The specificity of the blessing was underscored by the transgenerational repetition of the same promise to Isaac: "In you and in your descendants all the families of the earth shall be blessed."[2] The repeated reference to families underscores God's ongoing blessing of the foundational unit of society, the family. The blessing that God gave to Abraham's family was to be extended to the entire world, and the fundamental channel for the impartation of that blessing was to be the family.

God himself created the family in the Garden of Eden. He observed that it was not good for Adam to be alone; therefore, he formed Eve and began the institution of the family. From that moment to the present day, the family has been the locus for spiritual development and blessing. More than a mere social convention, the family is the earthly manifestation of the heavenly family. God is man's father, and heavenly Jerusalem "is the mother of us all."[3] In human families, God's will is done on earth as in heaven.[4]

A clear understanding of this truth was central to the Hebrew people who valued their families highly and maintained respect for parents, spouses, and children. The family was the unit for nurturing and strengthening individuals, as both husbands and wives profited from the balance of their relationship and children were nurtured in the security of a stable, loving environment and in the knowledge of the Lord.

Even when Israel had a sanctuary, whether the tabernacle in the wilderness or the temple in Jerusalem or the abundant synagogues in post-exilic times, the family remained the center of Hebrew life. Sarah and Abraham's tent was the pattern for the tabernacle and the temple. Later, the synagogues were mere extensions of the family.[5] The nuclear family of father, mother, and children was expanded to include the community and even the entire nation of Israel. No Hebrew thought of himself in purely individualistic terms. He was part of a family.

The earliest followers of Jesus continued this emphasis on family and the synagogue of extended family. It was altogether a part of the community of Judaism in the first century and maintained respect for Jewish values and applications. When Christianity emerged from the sect of Judaism that had been called the *Notzrim* (the followers of Jesus, the *netzer* or shoot from the stem of Jesse), it began to crystallize into a movement where focus was taken from the family and placed on the clergy. When Christendom developed, husbands and fathers were emasculated: their role of leadership in spiritual matters was eroded as it was arrogated to the church's priesthood. The church, not the family, became the center for salvation and blessing. Since that time, both the church and society have been impoverished by the loss of the biblically Hebraic focus on the family.

THE HOME AS SANCTUARY

In Hebrew thought, each home is viewed as a sanctuary. In Judaism the home is even termed a *mikdash me'at* (a mini-sanctuary). Indeed, every home should be viewed as a sanctuary from the world, a place of retreat into the safety of loving relationships and secure knowledge that God is present and maintains his blessings upon the family. In the mad rush for survival in a challenging world, everyone needs a sanctuary every day of life. A few hours each week in a corporate sanctuary called a "church" are not sufficient to meet human needs.

The *mikdash me'at* is a holy institution that is parallel with the dwelling place of God in both tabernacle and temple. The home is the fundamental abode of the Almighty. It is for this reason that the entrance to each Jewish home is marked with God's instructions for life that are affixed to the doorpost in the form of a *mezuzah*. The table, which is viewed in most Gentile homes as a vehicle for the distribution and consumption of food, is for the Jewish people a sacred altar, parallel with the altar in the temple. Around that altar the family gathers to worship their Father and King, to nurture one another, and to experience the reenactment of God's blessing on Abraham and on the ancient Israelites.

The idea that the table in the home is an altar is found in Malachi's description of the temple altar as a table (*shulhan*).[6] Because the prophet identified God's altar as a table, the Jewish people have understood that their tables are mini-altars. Viewing the table in this manner has transformed it from an appliance for acquiring sustenance to a center for spiritual blessing. The family gathered around it is seen as a spiritual unit. The father or head of household assumes the role of priest, bringing God's prescribed blessings into the home and upon the family.

All the functions of the synagogue are manifest in the home. Those functions have become the three titles that refer to the synagogue: *Beth Knesset* (house of meeting), *Beth Midrash* (house of study), and *Beth Tefillah* (house of prayer). The Jewish home is a house of social interaction and mutually affirming relationships on a purely human level. Time is set aside for family. The home is also a house of study,

where God's Word is discussed and taught. The home is where
education in general is encouraged by example, where both
spiritual and secular knowledge are honored, and where study
is viewed as a high form of worship. The Jewish home is also
a house of prayer, a place where God is worshiped through
reading Holy Scripture, through song, blessing, and prayer.
The home was not patterned after the synagogue; the synagogue was merely an extension of the home, manifesting its
principles in the context of community.

THE CENTER FOR BLESSING

With the home viewed as not merely a secular social
convention but a holy place, it is easy to see how the Hebraic family became a center for blessing. The divine imperative for blessing upon the children of Israel has been
fulfilled in the Jewish home, with parents assuming the role
of priesthood to impart the commanded blessing on their
children: "This is the way you shall bless the children of
Israel. . . ."[7] The blessing has been expanded to include other
biblical elements and has become a much-anticipated weekly
event in Jewish homes.

The prime importance that the Hebrews attached to
domestic life was reinforced by the mutual respect that was
maintained between parents and children. Children honored their parents even before it became a requirement of
the Decalogue; therefore, they placed high value on the favor of their parents. This was especially true of parental
blessings which both parents and children believed had profound power to produce good. In Hebrew culture, family
blessings were highly prized, even considered the most valu-
able heritage that parents could bequeath to their children.
The author of the apocryphal book of Ecclesiasticus observed
that "the blessing of the father builds houses to the sons."[8]

That the blessing in the context of family was a central part of Jewish life in biblical times is confirmed in the
experience of David. Immediately after the king of Israel

had led one of the most exhilarating corporate worship exercises of his life, he immediately retired to his home for the express purpose of blessing his family. David had just danced with all his might before the ark of the covenant that he had returned to prominence in Israel's worship experience. What a profound public demonstration of passionate devotion to the God of Israel! David's thoughts, however, were not lost in an ecstatic exercise of public worship, a momentary existential experience. His focus was on his family: "David returned to bless his household."[9]

Even though there were priests in Israel who were specifically commissioned with the responsibility to bestow God's blessing over the children of Israel, David remembered his primary role as the leader of his household and returned from a great exercise of public worship to the sanctuary of his home so he could bless his family. David's home, not the congregation or its establishment for religion, was the center of blessing and personal devotion.

SHABBAT, THE BLESSING THAT BLESSES

In order to facilitate the impartation of the blessing in the context of the family, the Creator set apart one day of the week as a time for God and family. This day was called the Sabbath. God established a pause in the hectic exercise of work, a sanctuary in time where his children could enjoy *menuach* (rest, repose). The sages wondered about the statement in Scripture that "on the seventh day God finished the work that he had been doing."[10] What did God create on the seventh day? The answer was that God created *menuach*.

God did not create a material sanctuary, a temple to which Adam and Eve and their descendants could resort for repose from their activities of life. He created a sanctuary in time that could be entered in any environment. The Sabbath was designed as a weekly sanctuary of remembrance, to focus man on the things in life that are really important: God and family. That is why the Sabbath commandment is the only instruction of the Decalogue that begins, "Remember. . ." Human beings are forgetful; therefore, they need a reminder. The Sabbath is just such a memory device that waves a red flag and sounds the alarm: "Stop! Take time for God and family."

It has been said that Israel has not so much kept the Sabbath as the Sabbath has kept Israel. This has been especially true in the fact that Sabbath is a family celebration. Though in the Christian world the one day in seven that has been set apart for God is viewed more as an opportunity for corporate worship, the Sabbath among the Jews is first a family exercise that is expanded into corporate worship. It is in the context of family intimacy that meeting, study, and prayer functions are fulfilled.

The Sabbath is the only immaterial thing that God ever blessed.[11] Like Abraham, the Sabbath was blessed so that it could be a blessing. It is a blessed time that sets apart a weekly occasion for blessing in the context of family and community. For millennia, therefore, millions of Jews have anxiously awaited *Shabbat* as the blessing that blesses.

BLESSING AFTER BLESSING

Shabbat begins on Friday evening at sundown and continues until Saturday evening.[12] In the Jewish home, the Sabbath is welcomed by the entire family, with the wife and mother having the honor of speaking the blessing and lighting the candles that usher in the Sabbath.

Along with other spiritual exercises that include reading God's Word and singing Psalms, the family's attention is focused on what has been awaited all week, the family blessings. The parents, with the father generally taking the leading role, place the blessing that God commanded for the children of Israel on each one of their own children individually. Because Jacob laid his right hand on Ephraim's head when he blessed him, the Jewish father lays his right hand on the head of each child as he speaks the blessing.[13]

This blessing involves the combination of both the Aaronic blessing and other scriptural and personal blessings.

The blessing is introduced by statements that originate in classic biblical blessings. If the child is male, the words that Jacob commanded for the blessing are spoken: "In your name will Israel pronounce this blessing, 'May God make you like Ephraim and Manasseh.' "[14] It is said that Jacob insisted that this blessing was to be pronounced upon all of Israel because the sons of Joseph were the first siblings who were never in conflict like their ancestors Cain and Abel, Jacob and Esau, and Joseph and his brothers. Because they worked together in harmony for the welfare of the family and community, they were to be paradigms of blessing for all future generations.

If the child is female, the words of the blessing that the leaders of the Israelite community placed upon Ruth are added: "The Lord make you like Sarah and Rebecca, Rachel and Leah."[15] Jewish girls are elevated in esteemed status to the rank of the women whom God used to establish the Hebrew peoples and the Israelite nation.

For both boys and girls, then, the blessing begins with the biblical declaration of benediction that was pronounced over their male and female ancestors. These statements connect children with the ancient patriarchs and matriarchs of the faith, building their self-esteem and giving them a sense of context in their extended family community. It invokes importance and accomplishment into their young lives and sets expectations for their future.

After the initial blessings, the process of blessing then continues with the impartation of the words that God commanded to be placed upon all the children of Israel: "The Lord bless you and keep you. The Lord make his face shine upon you and be gracious unto you. The Lord lift up his countenance upon you and give you peace." It may continue, "And they shall put my name upon the children of Israel, and I will bless them."

Afterwards a personal blessing can speak good things into each child's life, including parental expectations and affirmation of the child's life ambition and the parents' commitment to assist in fulfilling that ambition. Other blessings may be added as well. This is in keeping with the tradition of Jacob who "blessed [his children], every one with the blessing appropriate to him."[16] This confirms more than a routine blessing by rote. It is a personalized blessing that recognizes accomplishment and speaks positive expectation into the life of each child.

The blessing can continue with a petition for the sevenfold Spirit of God to be upon each child: "May the Spirit of the Lord rest upon you, the spirit of wisdom, the spirit of understanding, the spirit of counsel, the spirit of might, the spirit of knowledge, and the spirit of the fear of the Lord."[17] Applying this blessing invokes the seven spirits that burn before God's throne[18] to be manifest in the child's life.

It is uncertain how ancient the Jewish practice of blessing children by this formula may be. Its earliest mention in extant literature is in *Brautspiegel*, a book published in Basel in 1602. The writer stresses the fact that children should be trained from infancy to value parental blessings: "Before the children can walk they should be carried on Sabbath and holidays to the father and mother to be blessed; after they are able to walk they shall go of their own accord with bowed body and shall incline their heads and receive the blessing."[19] The *Synagoga Judaica*, published in 1604, notes that on the Sabbath parents bless their children and teachers bless their pupils.[20] The blessing was a family affair and a part of the community of extended family.

Next, the husband blesses his wife by speaking, chanting, or singing over his wife the blessing of the woman of valor: "What a rare find is a capable wife! Her worth is far beyond that of rubies. . . . Many women have done well, but you surpass them all."[21] These words that "King

Lemuel's"[22] mother taught him were declared in the scriptural record to be prophetic,[23] a fact that adds much weight to the blessing. The Jewish people believe that this blessing was originally spoken by Abraham over Sarah and was subsequently transmitted orally through each generation. Whatever the case may be, speaking the Word of God over one's wife is a powerful dynamic. It blesses her. It establishes her husband's high esteem for her in the eyes of the children. Perhaps it is even more important in blessing the husband also, for he cannot repeat God's Words of blessing without being impacted himself.

Before the meal, the father makes the *Kiddush* blessing, sanctifying the occasion by praising God for creating the fruit of the vine. A cup of wine is elevated and these words are said: "Blessed are you, O Lord our God, King of the universe, who creates the fruit of the vine." After the hands have been washed, the appropriate blessing is recited: "Blessed are you, O Lord our God, Ruler of the universe. You have sanctified us with your commandments and enjoined on us the cleansing of the hands." Then when all are seated, the father takes two specially prepared loaves of bread, elevates them, and makes this declaration: "Blessed are you, O Lord our God, King of the universe, who brings forth bread from the earth." Both of these blessings come from antiquity, predating the first century. Jesus and his apostles most certainly prayed these blessings as is evidenced at the Last Supper, when Jesus took both bread and wine and blessed God when he initiated the ordinance of communion.[24]

After the family shares a meal, the father leads in the offering of blessings to God for the meal. The blessing after the meal is called the *Birkhat haMazon*.[25] Of all the benedictions in Jewish ritual, it is considered to be the oldest and most important because it is the only blessing that God specifically commanded all of Israel to practice: "When you have eaten and are full, then you shall bless the Lord your

God for the good land which he has given you."[26] In obedience to this instruction, the ancient Israelites prayed and
blessed only after they had eaten, not before. In later times,
however, the sages decided that blessings should be said
before eating in the context of the belief that nothing should
be enjoyed without first blessing God who made the provision.[27] The idea of blessing a meal before it is consumed is a
Christian practice that is rooted more in the neo-Platonic
idea that the material is evil and must be blessed. In history, it was also an attempt to pray over food that might be
unhealthy or contain some toxin.

The *Birkhat haMazon* was originally composed of three
blessings: for food, for the land, and for Jerusalem. The
blessing for food praises God for feeding all creatures,
thereby connecting Israel with all living things. The blessing for the land expresses praise to God for the abundant
land of Israel. The blessing for Jerusalem praises God as the
"rebuilder" of Zion, thanks him for Jerusalem, and petitions his mercy for Israel. These three blessings long pre-
date the Christian era. A fourth blessing was added in the
second century of the common era when the Jews were
granted permission to bury their dead after the Romans
crushed the revolt that had been led by the messianic pre-
tender, Bar Kochba. It is a benediction of God who is
"kindly and deals kindly with all."

The bestowing of blessings continues throughout the
Sabbath, with both family and communal worship in the context of community. As the day comes to an end, the family
again assembles for the *Havdalah* experience in which sorrow
is expressed for the ending of the Sabbath and incense is burned
to carry the sweet aroma of the Sabbath over into the beginning of a new week.

The entire *Shabbat* experience is one of blessing after blessing. Blessings are imparted that strengthen the
family bonds of mutual respect and honor. God is exalted in the context of the home, transforming it from a

mere shelter from the elements into a spiritual sanctuary of safety and blessing. In the blessed home, Solomon's observation is true: "A righteous man who walks in his integrity–How blessed are his sons after him."[28]

The impact of family blessings like these in Jewish homes is immeasurable. When recounting her childhood experiences of being blessed by her rabbi grandfather, Dr. Rachel Remen observed, "These few moments were the only time in my week when I felt completely safe and at rest."[29] If this were the only effect of the blessing, it would be reason enough for its impartation. The truth is, however, that the family blessing exercise has life-giving and lifelong benefits.

SPECIAL BLESSING OCCASIONS

Significant events in the life cycle of each person are occasions for blessing. This is especially true in the development of a child. Blessing should begin with the time when realization that conception has occurred to the end of the parent's allotted time on earth. Parents should never cease to bless their children.

One should speak words of blessing over the unborn child in its mother's womb. The blessing can petition divine protection and favor on both mother and child. Immediately after birth parents can bless their newborn child. In the Jewish community every son experiences the covenant of circumcision on the eighth day of his life. Christians can profit from this example by verbally blessing their infant children.

Parents have a significant opportunity to bless their children when they reach puberty and assume responsibility for their own actions. In Judaism, this experience is called *Bar Mitzvah* (son of the commandment) and in some communities is extended to girls as well in the *Bat Mitzvah* (daughter of the commandment). It is at the age of thirteen (twelve for girls) when the child comes of age. In the ceremony, the father publicly acknowledges that from this time forward he is no longer responsible for the child's actions.

This is likely the source of the Christian idea of the "age of accountability," the age at which a child becomes responsible before God for his actions.

This is a significant event, a rite of passage in the life of a child. Christians can recognize this important time by publicly blessing their children and recognizing their transition from childhood and dependency on their parents. A special blessing (beyond that which is weekly imparted in the context of family) can be spoken over the child to encourage the child at this milestone and affirm parental support as the child begins to make decisions for life.

One of the most important events in an individual's life is marriage, the making of a covenant between two people who will join in unity to share their lives together. It is the time of the creation of a new family, a new home. Parents should be carefully and prayerfully involved in this exercise. In ancient times, parents even chose the mates for their children. Certainly parents should advise their children in what is one of life's most important decisions. Then, children should want their parents to be involved in the ceremony that joins them covenantally with their mate. This is a significant opportunity for parents of both bride and groom to pronounce God's blessing and their own personal blessings over their children. The ceremony of marriage is enriched by the participation of parents in this, the one role that is assigned to them for life: blessing their children. The biblical blessing should be used, and additional blessings may be written into the liturgy for the event or may be given extemporaneously.

As children become adults, they have the privilege of continuing to receive their parents' blessings. There is never an age when they outgrow the blessing. At the same time, however, children have the opportunity to rise up and call their parents blessed,[30] to honor their father and mother[31] both in word and deed and to reciprocate the blessings that they have received from their parents by blessing them in turn.

When one reaches full age and is ready to be "gathered to his ancestors," this is an important time for the intimacy of the family to be manifest in blessing. A patriarch or matriarch will want to add God's blessing to children and grandchildren and to hear words of blessing from their most precious possessions as they face the unknown but certain experience of death, burial, and resurrection.

Family blessing, then, is a lifetime affair. A blessed family never misses an opportunity for blessing one another. It is the heritage from the Lord, who is the source of all blessing.

BLESSING BY FAITH

Because Christians have not been accustomed to the biblical function of the home as the center for spiritual development, they are often uncomfortable with assuming the role of leadership in blessing. Their codependency upon the clergy as the official channels of blessing has robbed them of this privilege. In many cases, the church has eviscerated the home of this, its most important function. Those who have come to realize the extent of their impoverishment through the loss of this important part of Christianity's Hebraic heritage can now reclaim their rights and privileges.

Generational inhibitions, however, can restrict the freedom to engage in what is clearly a parental responsibility. Because one's parents have not fulfilled this role is no excuse for not taking on the challenge. Because one is not

Graphic from *Restore!* Magazine

Jewish fathers and grandfathers often bless the children under the the canopy of their prayer shawls.

fluent in verbal expression is also not an excuse. Perhaps what
is needed is the faith to bless.

When discussing the subject of faith, most Christians'
attention goes immediately to Hebrews 11, the one chapter
in the Apostolic Scriptures that is often referred to as the
"Hall of Fame of Faith." Here men and women of amazing
faith are chronicled, along with some of the astounding results of their faith. There is Enoch who was translated so as
not to experience death. There is Noah who built an ark
and saved humanity from the deluge. There are Abraham
and Sarah who experienced the miraculous birth of Isaac.
There is Moses who effected the Israelites' deliverance from
Egyptian bondage and experienced astounding miracles in
the process. There are Gideon, Samson, David, and Samuel,
all of whom witnessed supernatural intervention that impacted the nation of Israel.

Two men are mentioned in this illustrious list, however, simply because they had the faith to bless their children: "*By faith* Isaac blessed Jacob and Esau in regard to their
future. *By faith* Jacob, when he was dying, blessed each of
Joseph's sons"[32] (emphasis added). The faith that both Isaac
and Jacob manifest was equal to the faith that routed armies,
divided the Reed Sea, preserved Noah's ark, and established
prophets' words. It was faith that inspired these men to pro-
pel their values like arrows into the next generation in the
form of blessings for their children and grandchildren.[33]

Should Christians who are filled with the Holy
Spirit not have faith of the same caliber as that of Isaac
and Jacob? Perhaps it is time to take the faith which one
believes can move mountains and apply it to blessing
one's children. It may seem like a leap of faith for some,
but it is merely a step of obedience to God's command:
"Bless the children of Israel." Without such a step of
faith, one will experience the sorrow that Rachel Remen's
mother noted when asked why she had not blessed her
daughter: "I have blessed you every day of your life. . . .

I just never had the wisdom to do it out loud."[34]

Fixed forms of blessing that the Jewish people have used for generations may be shared in the context of Christian families. Self-composed or spontaneous expressions may also be used. If nothing else, as a Christian, be Christ-like: let it be said of you that you took your children up in your arms, "laid [your] hands on them, and blessed them."[35] Whatever the case, by faith–and by all means–bless your children.

OUTLINE FOR FAMILY BLESSINGS

When you as a Christian family gather together for the time set apart for God and family, you may wish to use the following outline as a guide for blessing both God and your family. This formula is similar to what has been done in Jewish homes for centuries. We have added language that expands the exercise to include various Christian elements.

At sundown, the mother may light candles and make the following blessing:

"Blessed are you, O Lord our God, King of the universe, who has sanctified us by your Word and has commanded us to be lights in the world. We thank you for your Son our Lord, Jesus the Christ, who has illuminated our lives with his divine presence and has given us your Holy Spirit."

The parents, with the father generally taking the leading role, now place the blessing that God commanded to be spoken over the children of Israel on each of their children. The Aaronic Blessing is introduced by scriptural blessings appropriate to sons and daughters. Parents may lay their hands on the head of each child individually and make the following blessing:

"May the Lord make you like Ephraim and Manasseh" (if the child is a boy).

"May the Lord make you like Sarah and Rebecca, Rachel and Leah" (if the child is a girl).

The blessing continues with this scripturally mandated personal blessing from God:

"The Lord bless you and keep you. The Lord make his face shine upon you and be gracious unto you. The Lord lift up his countenance upon you and give you peace."

You may continue:

"With this blessing, God said, 'I will put my name upon the children of Israel, and I will bless them.'"

Now, as Jacob did centuries ago, you should speak into each child's life a personal blessing that is appropriate to the child. This can express your thanks for the child's accomplishment as well as your expectations for the child's future. This should amplify the child's vision and ambition for life.

The blessing can then continue with the invocation of the sevenfold Spirit of God upon the child:

"May the Spirit of God rest upon you, the spirit of wisdom, the spirit of understanding, the spirit of counsel, the spirit of might, the spirit of knowledge, and the spirit of the fear of the Lord. And may you always delight in the fear of the Lord."

Next, the husband blesses the wife by reading or reciting all or part of Proverbs 31:10-31:

"A wife of noble character who can find? She is worth far more than rubies. Her husband has full confidence in her and lacks nothing of value. She brings him good, not harm, all the days of her life. . . . She sets about her work vigorously . . . She opens her arms to the poor and extends her hands to the needy. . . . She speaks with wisdom, and faithful instruction is on her tongue. She watches over the affairs of her household and does not eat the bread of idleness. Her children arise and call her blessed; her husband also, and he praises her: 'Many women do noble things, but you surpass them all.' Charm is deceptive and beauty is fleeting; but a woman who fears the Lord is to be praised. Give her the reward she has earned, and let her works bring her praise at the city gate."

The wife may also bless her husband by reading or reciting Psalm 112:1-9:

"Blessed is the man who fears the Lord, who finds great

delight in his commands. His children will be mighty in the land; the generation of the upright will be blessed. Wealth and riches are in his house, and his righteousness endures forever. Even in darkness light dawns for the upright, for the gracious and compassionate and righteous man. Good will come to him who is generous and lends freely, who conducts his affairs with justice. Surely he will never be shaken; a righteous man will be remembered forever. He will have no fear of bad news; his heart is steadfast, trusting in the Lord. His heart is secure, he will have no fear; in the end he will look in triumph on his foes. He has scattered abroad his gifts to the poor, his righteousness endures forever; his horn will be lifted high in honor."

Before the meal, the father takes a cup of wine and offers the same *Kiddush* blessing that Jesus and the apostles made:

"Blessed are you, O Lord our God, King of the universe, who has created the fruit of the vine." He may continue: *"We thank you for the blood of your Son that cleanses us from all iniquity."*

In like manner, the father takes two specially prepared loaves of bread and makes another blessing that Jesus made:

"Blessed are you, O Lord our God, King of the universe, who brings forth bread from the earth." He may continue: *"We thank you for your Son, the bread of life from heaven who strengthens our souls."*

The family shares a meal together at which there may be singing and sharing of God's Word. In the course of the meal, they may discuss the significance of the foods on the table that date from Bible times: bread, wine, oil, and salt, all of which have great spiritual significance.

When the meal is concluded, the family may join in blessing God for the foods. This is in obedience to God's command that the children of Israel were to bless the Lord after they had eaten and were full. The following *Birkhat haMazon* blessing dates from before the time of Jesus:

The father says: *"Let us say grace."* The rest of the family responds: *"Blessed be the Name of the Lord from this time forth and for ever."* The father continues: *"We will bless him of whose bounty we have partaken."* The family responds: *"Blessed be he of whose bounty we have partaken and through whose goodness we live."*

The family together may say all or part of the following blessing, the *Birkhat haMazon*:

"Blessed are you, O Lord our God, King of the universe, who feeds the whole world with your goodness, with grace, with loving kindness and tender mercy; you give food to all flesh, for your loving kindness endures for ever. Through your great goodness food has never failed us: O may it not fail us for ever and ever for thy great Name's sake, since you nourish and sustain all beings, and do good unto all, and provide food for all thy creatures whom you have created. Blessed are you, O Lord, who gives food to all.

"We thank you, O Lord our God, because you gave as a heritage unto our fathers a desirable, good, and ample land . . . and for the food wherewith you do constantly feed and sustain us on every day, in every season, at every hour. For all this, O Lord our God, we thank and bless you, blessed be your Name by the mouth of all living continually and for ever, even as it is written, And you shall eat and be satisfied, and you shall bless the Lord your God for the good land which he has given you. Blessed are you, O Lord, for the land and for the food.

"Have mercy, O Lord our God, upon Israel your people, upon Jerusalem your city, upon Zion the abiding place of your glory, upon the kingdom of the house of David, and upon the great and holy house that was called by your Name. O Lord our God, our Father, feed us, nourish us, sustain, support and relieve us, and speedily, O Lord our God, grant us relief from all our troubles. We beseech you, O Lord our God, let us not be in need either of the gifts of mortals or of their loans, but only of your helping hand, which is full, open, holy, and ample, so that we may never be put to shame or humili-

ated. And rebuild Jerusalem the holy city speedily in our days. Blessed are you, O Lord, who in your compassion rebuilds Jerusalem. Amen."

The family may conclude by praying the Lord's Prayer, after which the father may say, *"Now, may the grace of our Lord Jesus Christ, the love of God, and the fellowship of the Holy Spirit be with us all. Amen.*"

This concludes the *Shabbat* family blessing exercise.

[1] Genesis 12:3, NRSV.

[2] Genesis 28:14, NASB.

[3] Galatians 4:26.

[4] Matthew 6:10.

[5] The Jewish people understand that the tabernacle and the temple were fashioned after the pattern of Sarah and Abraham's tent.

[6] Malachi 1:7, 12.

[7] Numbers 6:23.

[8] Ecclesiasticus (Sirach) 3:9.

[9] 2 Samuel 6:20.

[10] Genesis 2:2, TNK.

[11] Exodus 20:11.

[12] In biblical terms, the day begins at sundown so that evening precedes morning and a day is defined as "evening and morning," even as the Genesis creation record declares.

[13] Genesis 48:17.

[14] Genesis 48:20.

[15] Ruth 4:11.

[16] Genesis 49:28, NASB.

[17] Isaiah 11:1.

[18] Revelation 4:5.

[19] Moses Henochs, *Brautspiegel*, quoted in "Blessing of Children," *JewishEncyclopedia.com*, p. 3.

[20] *Ibid.*, p. 3.

[21] Proverbs 31:10-31, TNK.

[22] It is thought that Lemuel may well be a term of endearment for Solomon himself.

[23] Proverbs 31:1.

[24] Matthew 26:26-27.

[25] *Mazon* means "foods."

[26] Deuteronomy 8:10.

[27] Babylonian Talmud, *Berakhot* 35a.

[28] Proverbs 20:7, NASB.

[29] Rachel Naomi Remen, *My Grandfather's Blessing* (New York: Riverdale Books, 2002), p. 48.

[30] Proverbs 31:28.
[31] Exodus 20:12.
[32] Hebrews 11:20-21.
[33] Psalm 127:4.
[34] Remen, p. 88.
[35] Mark 10:16.

Chapter 16

Ultimate Blessing

From the onset of creation, God has willed blessing upon humanity in general and on those who have approached him in faith in particular. From the beginning, belief in God has been belief that he is a rewarder of those who diligently seek him.[1] God's pursuit of men and women whom he can bless has been relentless. He has moved all of heaven and earth to fulfill his determination to bless, and countless millions have benefited from his benediction.

Because God is eternally present, he has been able to declare man's end from the beginning.[2] What was begun in original blessing will conclude in ultimate blessing. This is the promise of the Father to his children: the descendants of Abraham, both biological and spiritual, will be blessed throughout all their generations by the unilateral covenant that has made them God's chosen people. Because of the security of this immutable and inviolable oath,[3] the future for God's people is secure and bright!

Some have suggested that mankind is in the process of devolution, with matters going from bad to worse, with evil ever expanding its stranglehold on the masses, and with an ominous cloud of defeat hanging over humanity. While it is true that the apocalyptic literature of the Scriptures predicts times of trouble, famine, war, death, and de-

struction, these events and circumstances are only inter-
ludes between the provision for blessing that was made
when Jesus died on Mt. Calvary and the full realization
of blessing when he returns to the Mount of Olives. The
blessing of the believers is the expectation of resurrection unto eternal life in Christ's glorious kingdom when
the earth will be full of the glory of the Lord. "Blessed
be the God and Father of our Lord Jesus Christ, who
according to his abundant mercy has begotten us again
unto a living hope through the resurrection of Jesus
Christ from the dead."[4]

OPTIMISTIC ESCHATOLOGY

The Jewish people have long believed that prayer and
blessings lead to the redemption of the world. This is first
an ongoing effort of continual world restoration (*tikkun
olam*) in which man works in partnership with God through
prayer and blessings to the improvement of the world in
each generation. It is also an expectation of the *olam ha-ba*
(the world to come), the messianic age when everything
earthly will be restored to the pristine state of purity that
was manifest in the Garden of Eden. Everything will be
returned to its original state, including the global ecology,
economy, government, and religion. This optimistic
eschatology is the feature of Peter's post-Pentecost declaration that the Messiah would be received in heaven until the
time of the restoration of all things spoken by the prophets
since beginning of the world.[5]

The future is one of renewal both for God's elect and
for the earth. The universal restoration will be one of the
greatest expressions of divine blessing that the world has
ever seen. The blessing that was intended in the beginning
will be fully manifest in the end. God's will will be fully
accomplished in the earth as it is in heaven.

Part of the Jewish expectation for the redemption of
the world is based in their understanding that the Festival

of Tabernacles is a universal celebration in which God welcomes all men, Jew and Gentile, to the fellowship of his table. The sages have suggested that the Gentiles were included in the Tabernacles celebration because the 70 bulls that were sacrificed then corresponded to the 70 nations produced by the direct descendants of Noah.[6] This confirms the fact that all the nations of the world will experience God's redemption and salvation in the time of Messiah. The words of the prophets declare that the nations will be accepted on God's altar and will be blessed.[7] Jesus confirmed that God's sheep who were not in the fold of Israel would be gathered unto him.[8] The righteous of all the nations of the world, both Jew and Gentile, will stand with King Messiah on the Mount of Olives at the day of his return. The Lord shall be king over all the earth, and his name shall be one.[9] The *Shema* will be the all-encompassing word of Christ's eternal kingdom.

The salvation of the nations was made sure in the words of Jesus: "This gospel of the kingdom will be preached in the whole world as a testimony to all nations, and then the end will come."[10] The good news that is so powerful that even the gates of hell cannot resist[11] is destined to be heralded into all the world before the end of the age.[12] While the days of Messiah will be a time of trouble as evil foments itself in the earth and vaunts itself against the knowledge of God, the gospel is irrepressible and will not return void to him who has cast it like bread upon the waters of humanity.[13] Could it be that Paul's statement regarding the submission of the world when "every knee will bow and every tongue confess that Jesus is Lord"[14] may speak of a profound global revival that will turn the hearts of fathers to children and children to fathers[15] in a final denouement of the age of man?

KING MESSIAH'S COMING

The expectation of the Messiah's coming has sprung from the hearts of millions of Jews for more than three millennia while the hope of the Messiah's return has filled the hearts of multiplied millions of Christians over the past two thousand years. This is the blessed hope[16] that is woven like a scarlet thread through the very fabric of Holy Scripture. The first promise of Scripture is Messianic,[17] and it's last promise is Messianic.[18] The continuing expectation of this blessed event is secure in God's domain. The Messiah is destined to arrive on planet Earth at God's set time, just as his first coming was in the fullness of time.[19] Nothing that the forces of evil can marshal can delay that appointed time. God's appointments for the future are as certain and secure as his *mo'edim* (set times) of the past.

The believer need not fear the curses of the enemy, for they will be swallowed up in victory by the one whose eternal mission it has been to bless his covenant people with all blessings in heavenly places in Christ Jesus.[20] The shouts of victory that echoed through the hills of Judaea two thousand years ago will again resound in that land when the redeemed of the earth cry: "Blessed is the coming kingdom of our father David. . . . Hosanna in the Highest!"[21]

The promise of blessing that God made to King David will be fully realized when the Son of David returns in the same Judaean body[22] in which he lived on earth two millennia ago and sits on the throne of David to establish God's dominion over all the earth. The fullness of the seed of Abraham will bring to complete fruition the blessing promised to Abraham that his children will inherit the world.

EVEN SO, COME, LORD JESUS

"Blessed is the Lord God of Israel, for he has visited and redeemed his people . . . and remember[ed] his holy covenant, the oath which he swore to our father Abraham: to grant us that we . . . might serve him . . . in holiness and righteousness before him."[23] Then, "the kingdom and dominion . . . shall be given to the people, the saints of the Most High. His kingdom is an everlasting kingdom, and all dominions shall serve and obey him."[24]

The promise of Jesus is, "Behold, I come quickly."[25] The prayer on the lips of Jew and Christian alike is, "May the Messiah come speedily and in our lifetime." All of creation groans together awaiting this day,[26] and believers of all ages echo the prayer, "Even so come, Lord Jesus."[27] When the Messiah of Israel and the Savior of the world will be king over all the earth, he will say to his elect: "Come you who are blessed by my Father, take your inheritance, the kingdom prepared for you since the creation of the world."[28]

What God intended for humanity in the beginning will be fully realized in the end. Redeemed by the blood of the spotless Lamb, Adam and Eve's progeny will have dominion over all the earth, ruling with the Messiah in his everlasting kingdom. God's original blessing will become God's ultimate blessing, for the circle of mutual blessing–the essence of the kingdom–will find ultimate fulfillment in the Messianic Kingdom of the age to come.

Barukh haba b'Shem Adonai (Blessed is he who comes in the name of the Lord). *Barukh attah, Adonai Elohenu, Melekh haOlam . . . Barukh Shem k'vod malkhuto l'Olam va'ed!* (Blessed are you, O Lord our God, King of the universe . . . Blessed be the Name of his glorious kingdom for ever and ever!)

[1] Hebrews 11:6.
[2] Isaiah 46:10.
[3] Hebrews 6:13-14.
[4] 1 Peter 1:3.
[5] Acts 3:20-21.
[6] The descendants of Noah's three sons were said to be for languages and nations. They numbered exactly 70 according to Genesis 10.
[7] Isaiah 60:3, 8.
[8] John 10:16.
[9] Zechariah 12:1-10.
[10] Matthew 24:14.
[11] Matthew 16:18.
[12] Mark 13:10.
[13] Isaiah 55:11.
[14] Philippians 2:10.

[15] Malachi 4:6.
[16] Titus 2:13.
[17] Genesis 3:15.
[18] Revelation 22:20.
[19] Galatians 4:4.
[20] Ephesians 1:3.
[21] Mark 11:10, NIV.
[22] Acts 2:30.
[23] Luke 1:68-71, NIV.
[24] Daniel 7:27.
[25] Revelation 22:20.
[26] Romans 8:24.
[27] Revelation 22:20.
[28] Matthew 25:34.

Index

A

Aaronic Blessing 49, 162
Adonai 54, 56, 58
Aggadot 16
Aleph & *Tav* 22
Alpha & *Omega* 22
Amidah 82
Anointing 122
Appointment 121
Arminius, Jacobus 36
Augustine 33-36

B

Balaam 104-106, 134
Bar Mitzvah 157
Barak 93, 94
Bat Mitzvah 157
Beged 44
Berakhoth 13, 79, 83
Beth Knesset 149
Beth Midrash 149
Beth Tefillah 149
Birkhat haMazon 84, 155-156, 163-164

Blessing at Puberty 157
Blessing Children 50, 123, 150-162
Blessing Husbands 162-163
Blessing Wives 154, 162

C

Calvinism 35
Charis 72-77
Charismata 74, 77
Charity 73
Chesed 19, 27, 42, 72, 83, 94
Chosen People 15, 133-135
Chutzpah 20, 141
Cohanim 55
Curse Reverse 106
Curses 23, 102, 134-136

D

Deference 19
Delight 66, 130
Dualism 26, 34

Hebraic Heritage Christian Center

Hebraic Heritage Christian Center is an institution of higher education that is dedicated to the vision of restoring a Hebraic model for Christian education. A consortium of scholars, spiritual leaders, and business persons, the Center features a continually developing curriculum in which each course of study is firmly anchored in the Hebrew foundations of the Christian faith.

The Hebraic Heritage Christian Center vision combines both the ancient and the most modern in an educational program that conveys knowledge, understanding, and wisdom to a world-wide student population. The Center seeks to restore the foundations of original Christianity in order to equip its students with historically accurate, theologically sound understanding of the biblical faith that Jesus and the apostles instituted and practiced. At the same time the Center endeavors to implement the finest in innovative, cutting-edge technology in a distance-learning program that delivers its user-friendly courses by the Internet.

Among the wide range of services and products that Hebraic Heritage Christian Center offers are the publications of Hebraic Heritage Press. These are delivered both in traditional print media as well as in electronic media to serve both the Center's student population and the general public with inspiring and challenging materials that have been developed by the Center's team of scholars.

Those who are interested in sharing in the development of Hebraic Heritage Christian Center and its commitment to restoring the Jewish roots of the Christian faith are invited to join the Founders' Club, people who support this team of scholars and leaders by becoming co-founders of this institution. Many opportunities for endowments are also available to those who wish to create a lasting memorial to the cause of Christian renewal and Christian-Jewish rapprochement.

Hebraic Heritage Christian Center

P. O. Box 450848 ✡ Atlanta, GA 31145-0848
www.hebraiccenter.org

Get Your <u>Free</u> Copy of

The Magazine That's Restoring the Biblically Hebraic Heritage to Christian Believers Around the World

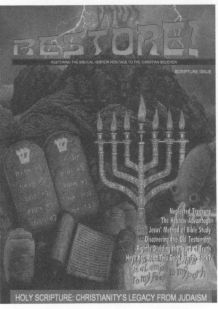

HOLY SCRIPTURE: CHRISTIANITY'S LEGACY FROM JUDAISM

Restore! is the exciting new journal that's. . .

✡ *helping Christians around the world to restore the Jewish roots of their faith in Jesus Christ.*

✡ *fighting against Judaeophobia, anti-Judaism, and anti-Semitism in the Christian church.*

✡ *encouraging Christians to support the international Jewish community and the nation of Israel.*

✡ *promoting unity (cohesiveness in the midst of diversity) within the universal body of Christ.*

HERE'S WHAT SOME OF OUR READERS ARE SAYING ABOUT *Restore!*

"I consider *Restore!* to be the best magazine on the restoration of Jewish roots because of its quality of presentation of the various topics, its scholarly articles, and most important, the strengthening of our faith that results the articles."—Michael Katritsis, Athens, Greece.

"*Restore!* is the best magazine I have ever read, the only one which I have read cover to cover."—Colyn King, Levin, New Zealand.

"*Restore!* is an inspiration both in its quality and the profundity of its contents."—Jorge Robles Olarte, Medellin, Columbia.

> ## Discover for yourself the Jewish roots of your faith as you read the informative, provocative material in the pages of *Restore!*

✂ -

❏ Please send me a free sample copy of *Restore!*
❏ Please enter my subscription to *Restore!* $25/yr. ($35 outside U.S.)
❏ Please bill my ❏Visa ❏American Express ❏Discover ❏MasterCard
#_____Exp._____
Name_____
Address_____
City_____State_____Code_____Nation_____

Restoration Foundation
P. O. Box 421218, Atlanta, GA 30342 E-Mail: info@restorationfoundation.org

Restore!

Restoration Foundation

P. O. Box 421218
Atlanta, GA 30342